STUDIES IN ECONOMIC AND SOCIAL HISTORY

This series, specially commissioned by the Economic History Society, provides a guide to the current interpretations of the key themes of economic and social history in which advances have recently been made or in which there has been significant debate.

Originally entitled 'Studies in Economic History', in 1974 the series had its scope extended to include topics in social history, and the new series title, 'Studies in Economic and Social History', signalises this development.

The series gives readers access to the best work done, helps them to draw their own conclusions in major fields of study, and by means of the critical bibliography in each book guides them in the selection of further reading. The aim is to provide a springboard to further work rather than a set of pre-packaged conclusions or short-cuts.

ECONOMIC HISTORY SOCIETY

The Economic History Society, which numbers over 3000 members, publishes the *Economic History Review* four times a year (free to members) and holds an annual conference. Enquiries about membership should be addressed to the Assistant Secretary, Economic History Society, Peterhouse, Cambridge. Full-time students may join at special rates.

STUDIES IN ECONOMIC AND SOCIAL HISTORY

Edited for the Economic History Society by L. A. Clarkson

PUBLISHED

W. I. *Albert* Latin America and the World Economy from Independence to 1930
B. W. E. *Alford* Depression and Recovery? British Economic Growth, 1918–1939
Michael Anderson Approaches to the History of the Western Family, 1500–1914
P. J. *Cain* Economic Foundations of British Overseas Expansion, 1815–1914
S. D. *Chapman* The Cotton Industry in the Industrial Revolution
Neil Charlesworth British Rule and the Indian Economy, 1800–1914
J. A. *Chartres* Internal Trade in England, 1500–1700
R. A. *Church* The Great Victorian Boom, 1850–1873
L. A. *Clarkson* Proto-Industrialization: The First Phase of Industrialization?
D. C. *Coleman* Industry in Tudor and Stuart England
P. L. *Cottrell* British Overseas Investment in the Nineteenth Century
Ralph Davis English Overseas Trade, 1500–1700
Ian M. Drummond The Gold Standard and the International Monetary System
M. E. *Falkus* The Industrialisation of Russia, 1700–1914
Peter Fearon The Origins and Nature of the Great Slump, 1929–1932
T. R. *Gourvish* Railways and the British Economy, 1830–1914
Robert Gray The Aristocracy of Labour in Nineteenth-century Britain, c.1850–1900
John Hatcher Plague, Population and the English Economy, 1348–1530
J. R. *Hay* The Origins of the Liberal Welfare Reforms, 1906–1914
R. H. *Hilton* The Decline of Serfdom in Medieval England
E. L. *Jones* The Development of English Agriculture, 1815–1973
John Lovell British Trade Unions, 1875–1933
W. J. *Macpherson* The Economic Development of Japan, c.1868–1941
Donald N. McCloskey Econometric History
Hugh McLeod Religion and the Working Class in Nineteenth-Century Britain
J. D. *Marshall* The Old Poor Law, 1795–1834
Alan S. Milward The Economic Effects of the Two World Wars on Britain
G. E. *Mingay* Enclosure and the Small Farmer in the Age of the Industrial Revolution
Rosalind Mitchison British Population Change Since 1860
R. J. *Morris* Class and Class Consciousness in the Industrial Revolution, 1780–1850
J. *Forbes Munro* Britain in Tropical Africa, 1870–1960
A. E. *Musson* British Trade Unions, 1800–1875
R. B. *Outhwaite* Inflation in Tudor and Early Stuart England
R. J. *Overy* The Nazi Economic Recovery, 1932–1938
P. L. *Payne* British Entrepreneurship in the Nineteenth Century
Roy Porter Disease, Medicine and Society in England, 1550–1860
G. D. *Ramsay* The English Woollen Industry, 1500–1750
Michael E. Rose The Relief of Poverty, 1834–1914
Michael Sanderson Education, Economic Change and Society in England, 1780–1870
S. B. *Saul* The Myth of the Great Depression, 1873–1896
Arthur J. Taylor Laissez-faire and State Intervention in Nineteenth-century Britain
Peter Temin Causal Factors in American Economic Growth in the Nineteenth Century
Joan Thirsk England's Agricultural Regions and Agrarian History, 1500–1750
Michael Turner Enclosures in Britain, 1750–1830
Margaret Walsh The American Frontier Revisited
J. R. *Ward* Poverty and Progress in the Caribbean 1800–1960

OTHER TITLES IN PREPARATION

The Cotton Industry in the Industrial Revolution

Prepared for
The Economic History Society by

S. D. CHAPMAN
Pasold Reader in Business History
University of Nottingham

Second Edition

MACMILLAN
EDUCATION

First Published 1972. Second Edition 1987

Published by
MACMILLAN EDUCATION LTD
Houndmills, Basingstoke, Hampshire RG21 2XS
and London
Companies and representatives
throughout the world

Printed in Hong Kong

British Library Cataloguing in Publication Data
Chapman, S. D.
The cotton industry in the Industrial
Revolution. — 2nd ed. — (Studies in
economic and social history).
1. Cotton manufacture — Great Britain —
History
I. Title   II. Series
338.4' 767721' 0941   HD9881.5
ISBN 0–333–45235–6

Series Standing Order

If you would like to receive future titles in this series as they are
published, you can make use of our standing order facility. To place a
standing order please contact your bookseller or, in case of difficulty,
write to us at the address below with your name and address and the
name of the series. Please state with which title you wish to begin your
standing order. (If you live outside the UK we may not have the rights
for your area, in which case we will forward your order to the publisher
concerned.)

Customer Services Department, Macmillan Distribution Ltd
Houndmills, Basingstoke, Hampshire, RG21 2XS, England.

Contents

Note on References   6

List of Tables   7

Editor's Preface   9

1   The Early Development of the Cotton Industry,
    1600–1760   11

2   Technology   17

3   Capital and Structure of the Industry   26

4   Commercial Organisation and Markets   36

5   Labour and Industrial Relations   45

6   The Role of Cotton in the Growth of the Economy   53

    References   62

    Select Bibliography   64

    Index   73

Note on References

References in the text within square brackets refer to the numbered items in the bibliography. Colons separate italicised page numbers from their appropriate references and semicolons separate different references.

List of Tables

I	Water and Steam Power in 1835	19
II	Labour Productivity in Cotton Spinning	20
III	Estimates of the number of and Fixed Capital invested in British Cotton Mills, 1787–1812	29
IV	Estimates of Fixed and Working Capital in the British Cotton Industry, 1834–56	29
V	Elements of Cost in the Price of Yarn, 1779–1812	37
VI	Total British Exports and Exports of British Cottons 1784–1856	43
VII	Export of Cotton Goods to 'Old' and 'New' Markets 1784–1856	43
VIII	Estimates of the Numbers of Domestic Workers in the Cotton Industry, 1795–1833	51
IX	Estimates of the Output of the Cotton Industry and its Contribution to National Income, 1760–1817	55
X	Number and Average Size of Cotton Mills in Britain, 1797–1850	60

Editor's Preface

WHEN this series was established in 1968 the first editor, the late Professor M. W. Flinn, laid down three guiding principles. The books should be concerned with important fields of economic history; they should be surveys of the current state of scholarship rather than a vehicle for the specialist views of the authors, and above all, they were to be introductions to their subject and not 'a set of pre-packaged conclusions'. These aims were admirably fulfilled by Professor Flinn and by his successor, Professor T. C. Smout, who took over the series in 1977. As it passes to its third editor and approaches its third decade, the principles remain the same.

Nevertheless, times change, even though principles do not. The series was launched when the study of economic history was burgeoning and new findings and fresh interpretations were threatening to overwhelm students – and sometimes their teachers. The series has expanded its scope, particularly in the area of social history – although the distinction between 'economic' and 'social' is sometimes hard to recognise and even more difficult to sustain. It has also extended geographically; its roots remain firmly British, but an increasing number of titles is concerned with the economic and social history of the wider world. However, some of the early titles can no longer claim to be introductions to the current state of scholarship; and the discipline as a whole lacks the heady growth of the 1960s and early 1970s. To overcome the first problem a number of new editions, or entirely new works, have been commissioned – some have already appeared. To deal with the second, the aim remains to publish up-to-date introductions to important areas of debate. If the series can demonstrate to students and their teachers the importance of the discipline of economic and social history and excite its further study, it will continue the task so ably begun by its first two editors.

The Queen's University of Belfast   L. A. CLARKSON
                                                General Editor

1 The Early Development of the Cotton Industry, 1600–1760

MOST of what is known about the early development of the cotton industry in Britain can be found in Wadsworth and Mann's *The Cotton Trade and Industrial Lancashire, 1600–1780*. It appears that the manufacture of cotton came to Britain from the Low Countries in the sixteenth century, one of the range of 'new draperies' that was transforming the textile industry in the later Tudor period. It was brought to East Anglia by Walloon and Dutch immigrants who settled in Norwich and other towns and established the manufacture of fustian, a mixture of linen with cotton imported from the Levant. Towards the end of the sixteenth century fustian reached Lancashire and began to oust the woollen industry from the western side of the county.

The developments that took place from this introduction to the middle of the eighteenth century cannot concern us in any detail. It is only possible to pick out the characteristics of the trade that emerged in this period and which help to explain its phenomenal success after that time. Three closely related subjects traced by Wadsworth and Mann require attention: the influence of London as a market and a supplier of raw materials and capital; the emergence of the domestic system of industrial organisation in Lancashire; and the part played by oriental influences on fashion and overseas trade generally.

Economic historians of the early period have rightly emphasised the important role of London in the national economy, calling on centres of regional specialisation both for the basic needs of its growing population and for the wealthy classes who were coming to regard it as proper to buy town houses and gather in the metropolis for the season. It was this growing market, fed, so far as textiles were concerned, through Blackwell Hall, that provided the major encouragement to the emergent manufacture in the seventeenth century. London dealers, often of Lancashire extraction, might employ an agent in Manchester to buy up cloth from the scattered manufacturers, or Manchester fustian dealers might forward goods to Blackwell Hall, the London cloth market, on their own account. Most of the raw cotton was imported through London and forwarded to Manchester on credit terms that encouraged the northern manufacturer. By the late seventeenth century the bill of exchange drawn on London had become the predominant means of payment for Lancashire dealers, and this financial support was crucial to the development of the trade.

London also played an important role in technical innovation in the cotton industry, acting as a nursery for techniques brought from the Continent or from India until they were ready for transplanting to the provinces, where there was less competition for land, labour and capital. Thus the 'Dutch engine loom', a complicated machine that made several linen or cotton tapes at once, found its way to Manchester via London. It was introduced by alien (probably Dutch) settlers early in the seventeenth century and was in use in Manchester by the Restoration. By 1750 there were at least 1500 Dutch looms in use in the parish of Manchester, concentrated in enlarged workshops distinct from the weavers' cottages, and Wadsworth and Mann recognise the Dutch loom workshops as a first step in the transition to the factory system.

The technique of printing fustians with bright-coloured designs was also a London industry before it migrated to the North-west to become the foundation of the Lancashire calico-printing industry. Most dyes available in the seventeenth century had a weak affinity for cotton, and the fundamental technique, copied from Indian craftsmen on the Malabar coast, was the application of mordants to fix the dye in the cloth so that it could be washed without losing its character. Calico printing was established in London by 1675 and soon began to achieve success in imitating the popular oriental designs; by 1712 'the East India Company was informing its agents that printing could be done in England at half the price charged for Indian goods and in better colours and patterns'. Unhappily this success aroused the enmity of the established woollen and silk industries, and during a prolonged agitation coinciding with the depression in trade caused by the outbreak of war with Spain in 1718, they succeeded in persuading Parliament to prohibit the sale, use and wear of English calicoes. However, the Act left two loopholes from which Lancashire was to benefit: it allowed calico printing for the export trade, and exempted the printing of fustians. In practice, English fustian was increasingly difficult to distinguish from Indian calico, and manufacturers took advantage of this similarity not only in the domestic market, but also in selling on the Continent, particularly in France, where calico printing had been banned in 1686.

The original role of Lancashire was to weave the fustian cloth which was sent to London for bleaching, printing and marketing. The fustian manufacturing process in the seventeenth and eighteenth centuries was organised on what is often called the domestic system. The entrepreneur was a merchant resident in Manchester, Bolton or Blackburn, and having trade connections with London. He distributed raw cotton and linen to a dispersed army of domestic spinners and weavers through local agents (or middlemen) called fustian manufacturers. The domestic workers were wage-earners, but they might own their own wheels and looms, and some drew support from farming activities [5:72–91, 314–23]. By the middle of the eighteenth century a large proportion of the population of Lancashire and the adjacent parts of the West Riding and Cheshire were dependent on the textile industry. Analysis of the baptismal registers shows that in the neighbourhood of Manchester from 50 to 70 per cent of the fathers recorded worked in some branch of the textile industries, while in Saddleworth (an area of some 40 square miles of gritstone Pennines between Oldham and Huddersfield) there were as many as 85 per cent.[1] The important point is that the Lancashire region saw the evolution of a capitalist class and an experienced workforce for nearly two centuries before the first water-powered cotton mills were built in the area. William Radcliffe of Mellor (near Stockport) recounted how a child brought up in a home where the cotton manufacture was carried on acquired 'a practical knowledge of every process from the cotton bag to the piece of cloth', and how such training laid the foundation for an independent career in the industry during the rapid growth of the trade in the 1780s and 1790s.[2]

There was a third innovation which was nourished in London for most of the seventeenth century before migrating to the provinces. The stocking frame was invented by the Revd William Lee, an obscure Renaissance genius who came from Calverton, a village just to the north of Nottingham, and took his complex

13

mechanism to London in the hope of obtaining royal support in 1589. He was disappointed, but his workmen settled in the capital and succeeded well enough to obtain a charter from Cromwell in 1657. Lee's frame was originally used to make silk and worsted stockings, but in 1732 a Nottingham workman succeeded in his attempts to knit cotton on the machine. By this time the East Midlands, which had retained some residual interest in the stocking frame after Lee left for London, were rapidly reasserting their right to the invention, offering cheaper labour and living costs, and freedom from the restricting ordinances of the chartered company. At the middle of the eighteenth century the merchant hosiers of Nottingham, Leicester, Derby and the satellite towns were employing large numbers of domestic framework knitters and, from small origins, were becoming a wealthy trading elite. Like the Lancashire merchants, they were still dependent on London for their market, but were becoming sufficiently independent to take the initiative in seeking both new techniques and new markets.[3]

London enterprise and capital also played the pioneer role in the early development of the factory system in the provinces. The earliest water-powered silk mill in Britain was built at Derby by Thomas Cotchett, a London silk reeler, following a lease of water rights on the Derwent in 1704. By 1707 Cotchett had installed '16 double Dutch mills', so it is possible that he was trying to apply power to the Dutch engine loom as well as to reeling silk. Cotchett's works proved expensive and were probably not successful technically; at any rate he became bankrupt in 1713 and the mill was released to Cotchett's friend John Lombe, who already had some silk-reeling machinery at work in London. Lombe and his half-brother Thomas Lombe, a wealthy London silk merchant, extended the works with the benefit of additional technical knowledge from Leghorn, where silk-reeling mills were already an important part of industrial structure. The Lombes succeeded in making the Derby silk mill pay its way, not only because John was well informed on the most up-to-date Italian technology, but also because, as manager, he succeeded in establishing a regimen of order and discipline for the 300 workers employed at the mill.[4] The buildings and organisation at Derby were copied in six mills at Stockport between 1732 and 1768, and in others at Congleton (1754), Macclesfield (1756), Sheffield (1768) and Watford (1769), and they exercised an influence over the development of the early factory system in the cotton industry, partly because Arkwright's Derby partner, Jedediah Strutt, consciously copied the organisation of the Derby mill, and partly because the mills at Stockport and Sheffield were converted to cotton in the early and still experimental period of Arkwright's success. The history of Stockport shows that the organising ability, inventive capacity and upward social mobility that came to be regarded as characteristic of cotton were found in the town's silk industry a generation earlier [48:23–9].

Up to this point the growth of the cotton industry has been analysed mainly from the supply side; it is now time to examine the problem of the increase in demand. Some reference has been made to the influence of oriental technique and design, and this can be examined first. Since Wadsworth and Mann completed their book, the historians of design have become keenly interested in the origins of printed textiles and their expertise has radically improved our understanding of the subject. In their *Origins of Chintz*, John Irwin and Katharine Brett show that the East India Company at first imported Indian fabrics only as novelties or curiosities, mainly using them as exchange in the spice trade with Malaya. However, by 1643 the Company's directors were beginning to realise the possibilities of the home market, and instructed their agents that the design of imported chintzes should respond to taste in the London market. By 1669 the directors were sending out patterns to be copied, and ordering 2000 pieces at a time. To keep pace with the accelerating demand, English and Dutch traders settled Indian cotton painters within the protected area of their own trading stations. British governments' attempts to restrict the calico trade in 1700 and 1720 never achieved total prohibition, and the competition of the East India Company's factories continued to present a challenge to English manufacturers to improve their craftsmanship until the end of the eighteenth century [63].

Some reference has already been made to the large export of printed cottons at the middle of the eighteenth century. For the first three-quarters of the century, until the new technology began to undermine the competitive position of Continental producers, most of the overseas demand came from Africa (where brightly printed cottons were exchanged for cargoes of slaves for the West Indian or Virginian plantations) and from the American and West

Indian colonists. As Wadsworth and Mann explain, this highly successful trade 'was prophetic of Lancashire's later pre-eminence in providing for warm climates and coloured races'. It was the carefully cultivated domestic and overseas market, rather than superior technology, that was the key to British achievement in the cotton industry until after the middle of the eighteenth century [5: Ch. 8].

In the second half of the eighteenth century a major shift in fashion, always a potent factor in the fortunes of the textile industry, gave new impetus to the rise of cotton. Down to the 1760s European fashions largely followed those of the French court at Versailles, featuring elaborate garments, with a profusion of ornate silks and ribbons. In the last 40 years of the century English fashions overtook the French, sober country simplicity conquering the expensive and impractical creations of the French court, with linens and cottons becoming increasingly popular for women's dresses and plain woollen cloths for men's wear. In this period ladies' magazines and pocket books already circulated widely, keeping the provinces in step with London fashions. Homogeneity of taste created a single national market for British textile manufacturers, while London fashion leadership extended that market to the Continent, the United States and the Colonies. As *The Magazine à la Mode* insisted in 1777, 'every variation of the fashions gives new life to trade, both in town and country' [62: *221*]. Fashions reached all classes of society as the upper classes distributed their cast-offs in the servants' hall and a large market in second-hand clothing developed. This fashion-conscious society was a major factor in the mechanisation of the cotton industry, for it was clear that every reduction in price of plain and printed cotton fabrics would find ever more eager buyers in the lower classes [57: *204–10*].

2 Technology

A GREAT deal of interest has attached to the mechanisation of the cotton industry because it is seen as a starting point of the modern technique of production that we call the factory system. Spinning was traditionally a simple handicraft consisting of only two motions, stretching then twisting the clean combed cotton fibres, and it proved relatively easy to imitate this activity with a machine. The earliest invention in economic use, James Hargreaves' spinning jenny, simply replicated the work of a number of spinners, and it was sufficiently small to be located in the workers' homes or in adjacent workshops [6:42–4]. The vital economic advance took place when this machine, and rivals invented or patented by Richard Arkwright and Samuel Crompton, had grown to a size that made manual operation too laborious. Power had to be introduced and the workers became machine minders rather than machine operatives [11:114–26; 16:176–9].

The father of modern economics, Adam Smith, showed in his *Wealth of Nations* (1776) how the greatest economies in manufacturing came from the 'division of labour', illustrating his idea with a factory that employed 16 different processes and workers to make pins. This form of manufacturing organisation, which has been called a proto-factory, also occurred in the early cotton industry, especially in calico printing [25:451–78]. When various forms of power – horses, water wheels, windmills and steam engines – were harnessed to the new spinning machines, along with their complementary cleaning, carding, roving and other processes, a new form of organisation was born, the fully-evolved factory. During the course of the nineteenth century, the power-driven (fully-evolved) factory gradually superseded the proto-factory in weaving, printing, knitting and other textile processes, and presently in a range of other industries. But before surveying the diffusion of cotton industry techniques to complementary and competing industries, we must examine the late eighteenth-century changes rather more closely.

Richard Arkwright and his partners had to instal a horse capstan in their first factory (a converted house in Nottingham) in 1769, and many of those who copied the technique at first used the same source of power. Horse capstans were cheap to instal (insurance records show that they were seldom valued at more than £50) and particularly suited to the stage at which small fustian manufacturers or hosiers were adapting existing premises to factory production, either for warp spinning (Arkwright's technique) or, a little later, for the carding engine and power-assisted mule. Horse capstans were indeed so common that few contemporaries thought them worthy of note, but scattered references suggest that they were possibly the most common kind of power installation until the end of the century, and formed an important stepping-stone from domestic to factory production [14: 47–9].

However this may be, there can be little doubt that water wheels provided most of the power for the cotton industry until after 1820. Early in the eighteenth century the traditional paddle (or 'undershot') water wheels began to be replaced by the more efficient breast and overshot wheels, particularly after John Smeaton, the most famous engineer of the age, demonstrated the increased power of the latter with experimental models in some lectures to the Royal Society in London in 1751.[5] The power requirements of the cotton industry were at first quite modest (it has been estimated that in 1795 the whole of the year's import of cotton could have been spun with 5000 h.p.) and, in the Pennines, where a typical minor stream draining into the Manchester embayment could generate more than 400 h.p., increased power demands appear to have been met without an immediate shortage of water power. Again, the importance of this factor is that costs were kept low during the crucial pioneer years, enabling entrepreneurs of limited resources to enter or retain a place in the industry.

By the middle of the eighteenth century the Newcomen steam engine was employed in most mining districts for drainage, and was soon at work replenishing reservoirs in locations of the textile industry where coal was plentiful and cheap. Local shortages of water power, especially on the Midland plain and the urban centres of the cotton industry, compelled factory owners who wanted to remain on the same site to consider the possibility of using James Watt's rotary steam engine in direct transmission to carding and spinning machinery. Several of the leaders of the industry, notably Arkwright, the Peels and Major Cartwright (brother of the inventor Edmund Cartwright), were involved in some costly failures with pioneer steam mills, and those who persevered complained of high maintenance costs, slow after-sales service and, above all, capital and running costs, much in excess of a water wheel on a good stream. The cost of power is very difficult to calculate for this period as data are scarce, and every water-power site involved the buyer or lessee in a different outlay and presented its own individual return to the investment; but such evidence as is available points to the conclusion that those occupying sites yielding more than 10 to 20 h.p. found them competitive until the late 1830s, when the efficiency of steam engines began to increase [8: *1–24*; 16, *204–24*].

Unfortunately, there are no general surveys of the comparative importance of water and steam power until 1835, when the steam engine, after more than half a century of continuous improvement, had become the predominant form of power in every cotton town in the North of England except a few Pennine centres like Glossop, Mottram and Halifax. By that time, as the figures in Table I show, steam was responsible for three-quarters of the power used in the industry. The table draws particular attention to the dominance of the Northern region (i.e. Lancashire and the adjacent parts of Cheshire, Derbyshire and the West Riding), which was clearly secured by steam power. At the end of the eighteenth century this region had contributed something like 70 per cent of the cotton manufacture; but in 1835 it had reached 90 per cent. Steam power was still as expensive as water power, but its

Table I   Water and Steam Power in 1835

	No. of mills	Steam h.p.	Water h.p.
Northern region	934	26,513	6,094
Scotland	125	3,200	2,480
Midlands	54	438	c. 1,200
Total	1,113	30,151	c. 9,774

Source: [1: *386–92*].

use was economised, partly by specialisation on manually operated power-*assisted* mules, partly by the increasing concentration of the cotton industry on the Lancashire coalfield. In the peripheral areas the older roller spinning technique of Arkwright, extravagant with the more abundant water-power resources of the Peak district and Scotland, continued to specialise on coarse spinning [36: 135−53]. However, these distinctions demand some basic appreciation of the nature of the two principal methods of production, and warrant closer examination.

The most important features of the introduction of mechanised carding and spinning are the spectacular increase in output, the fundamental improvement in quality of yarns, and the continuous trend of falling prices. The easiest way of illustrating the quantitive change is to reproduce the data on labour productivity in Catling's study of *The Spinning Mule*, where the modern concept of O.H.P. (i.e. the number of Operative Hours to Process 100 lb. of cotton) is applied to historical situations (see Table II). The only qualification that must be made to this table is that there was frequently a time-lag between the introduction of improved machinery and its widespread adoption. Catling's estimates do not cover the older (Arkwright) technique of roller spinning, but it is possible to make calculations from contemporary descriptions of mills. Specifications of the most efficient mills suggest that they fell within the 250−370 O.H.P. range in the 1780s and 1790s, i.e. that productivity was as high as in mule spinning during the pioneer years.[6] The labour force at Arkwright-type mills was mostly unskilled females and juveniles on low wages, while mules were operated by men whose skill was scarce and expensive, so that as long as the two systems could compete in quality, entrepreneurs with capital pursued the Arkwright system.

Table II   Labour Productivity in Cotton Spinning

Indian hand spinners (18th cent.)	50,000 + O.H.P.	
Crompton's mule (1780)	2,000	,,
100-spindle mule (*c.* 1790)	1,000	,,
Power-assisted mules (*c.* 1795)	300	,,
Roberts's automatic mules (*c.* 1825)	135	,,
Most efficient machinery today (1972)	40	,,

Source: [7: *54*].

The quality of yarn was the decisive factor in the competition between the rival systems. The traditional one-thread hand wheel spun 'little or no thread finer than 16 to 20 hanks in the pound, each hank measuring 840 yards', and evenness depended on the delicacy of touch of the spinner. (This degree of fineness – the count of the yarn – was expressed, by trade convention, as 16s to 20s, and other achievements *pro rata*.) Hargreaves's jenny, duplicating the motions of the hand spinner, reached the low 20s, while Arkwright, at the pinnacle of his achievement, attained 60s [6: 44]. Apart from calico printing, the competition was principally focused on quantity rather than quality up to this time. The manufacture of fine articles still depended on highly skilled workers, and the Swiss towns of Zürich, Wädenswil, Horgen, Stäfa and St Gall had practically the European monopoly; the only competition attempted was from the cambric manufacturers at St Quentin and Tarare, towards 1756, and Glasgow in 1769. Crompton's mule, which was soon spinning 80s, and reached 300s by the end of the century, transformed the situation almost overnight. Thomas Ainsworth at Bolton (1780) and Samuel Oldknow at Anderton and Stockport (1782–4) began making muslins, and three years later, in 1787, Britain already produced 500,000 pieces.

Lancashire success in the mechanisation of fine spinning not only absorbed the enterprise and capital of the region in the 1780s and 1790s, but also began to divert capital from Arkwright's system. By 1795, when M'Connel & Kennedy of Manchester succeeded in applying a Boulton & Watt steam engine to the two 'heavy' motions of the four-movement cycle of the mule, many of the pioneers of the Arkwright system, like the Peels and Douglases, began to direct their investment into the new and rapidly developing technique, though the older system (as Strutt's experience illustrates) continued to provide prosperity for a number of efficient firms. Consequently, mule spinning quickly superseded warp spinning in importance, and was the predominant system for the remainder of the period covered by this study. The only exception to this generalisation was the early 1830s, when investment in power looms, which were at first only suitable for the coarser yarns, led to a temporary revival of interest in warp spinning [18: 235–56].

Spinning by power commands more attention than any other

technique because it set in motion a sequence of technical and organisational changes in connected branches of the industry. Success at the spinning stage of the production process immediately created the need for an increase of output at the earlier stages, and all the important inventors of spinning machines were compelled to divert their minds to preparation machinery. The cotton from the bale had to be picked and cleaned, 'batted' (or beaten, to open the fibres), carded into a continuous sliver, 'drawn' (to lay the fibres parallel) and 'roved' (to attenuate the sliver) before it reached the spinning frames, and in the lifetime of Arkwright and Crompton a community of fertile minds in the Lancashire cotton towns succeeded in mechanising these processes. The outcome was the perfection of a system of continuous (or flow) production in which the cotton was mechanically handled from the moment the bales were hoisted from the drays to the top floor of the mill to that at which it was dispatched, in carefully graded yarns, from the ground-floor warehouse. Rapid dispersion of these ideas was the work of a corps of specialised millwrights and machine builders, who erected the mill buildings and machinery on uniform lines, originally imitating the achievements of Arkwright, Peel and other pioneers [14: 99; 9: 16].

The Hargreaves and Arkwright techniques of spinning superseded the old hand spinning wheels with a speed that, in retrospect, appeared almost dramatic. In 1768–9 there were some angry demonstrations in the Blackburn area by people who feared unemployment, but the general experience was probably reflected by William Radcliffe's comment on the change at Mellor (Stockport). 'The hands, turned adrift from hand cards and the spinning wheel, soon found full employ in the loom on machine yarn, with three to four fold more wages than they had been able to earn in their own trade', he recalled. Some families with no reserves of capital, Radcliffe infers, were forced out of the industry, but for those with initiative there was a golden opportunity to earn unprecedented wages and establish themselves as independent manufacturers.[7]

The rising costs that led to the era of inventions in the spinning section of the industry found a parallel in some other sections, particularly weaving, knitting, bleaching, dyeing and calico printing. Wadsworth and Mann wrote of a 'rapid transition to industrial capitalism' in these later stages of production between

1750 and 1780, and though they were evidently reviewing a variety of precocious enterprises rather than the typical firm, there can be no doubt that the period saw considerable growth in the size of workshops. Weaving looms and knitting frames were beginning to be concentrated in workshops employing supervised wage-earners, either to reduce the time wasted in distributing raw materials and collecting goods from domestic workers, or to improve the quality of the finished product. By the early nineteenth century, according to Bythell, there were isolated weaving sheds 'with as many as 150 or 200 handlooms, quite a few with between 50 and 100, and a considerable number with 20 or more. Such sheds were to be found in town and country throughout the weaving area.' This development, Bythell maintains, 'represented a half-way stage between true domestic industry and the modern power-driven weaving shed'. In the printing section of the industry there is also evidence of concentrations of labour and capital. The leviathan of the industry, Livesey, Hargreaves & Co. of Blackburn, employed about 900 workers shortly before their bankruptcy in 1788 [65: 33; 43: 29].

The traditional bleaching technique involved repeated immersions of the cloth in sour milk (lactic acid), followed by weeks of tentering in the open fields to allow the sun to complete the process. The whole process lasted seven or eight months in all. Dr John Roebuck's sulphuric acid plants in Birmingham (1746) and Prestonpans, Scotland (1749), inaugurated a sharp decline in the price of this industrial chemical, and it was soon replacing sour milk in bleaching, reducing the process to about four months. However, the most drastic economy of time, as a result of which bleaching lasted little more than a day, was not made until the end of the century. Charles Tennant of Glasgow, exploiting the discoveries of Berthollet, Scheele and pioneer plants in Manchester, Nottingham, Aberdeen and other centres of the cotton industry, successfully launched the commercial manufacture of bleaching powder. The new techniques called for specialised knowledge of chemistry, and bleaching powder manufacturers seldom had interests in spinning or weaving, though a few of them were also active as dyers and printers. Both bleachworks and dyeworks used water wheels through the period covered by this study, the former to power 'wash wheels' and 'dash wheels' (hammers to wash and pound the cloth free of acid), the latter to grind down dyewoods. Steam power was introduced to calico printing from about 1760, when Asterleys of Wandsworth installed 'a fire engine' at their printworks [12: *Ch. 8*; 25: *459*].

Weaving and knitting were technically more difficult to subject to the water wheel and steam engine, and when efficient machines were finally developed (in weaving in the 1830s, in knitting in the 1850s), their adoption was inhibited by the poor wages of handloom weavers and framework knitters. The earliest patents for a power loom were taken out by the Revd Edmund Cartwright in 1786–8, and he and his brother (Major John Cartwright) tried to develop the invention in factories at Doncaster and Retford (Notts.), but neither succeeded. Cartwright's loom was brought to commercial success by Radcliffe, Horrocks, Marsland and other Stockport manufacturers in the first years of the nineteenth century, but the general adoption of their looms was deferred until the investment booms of 1823–5 and 1832–4. In 1833 there were estimated to be 100,000 power looms in Britain, a number which can be compared with 250,000 handloom weavers [1: *228–40*]. Meanwhile a major new advance was taking place in mechanised spinning, and it was this and the power looms that dictated a multiplication of the scale of the most efficient factories.

The change in scale began in the middle 1830s with the widespread adoption of Roberts's automatic mule. In 1832 an expert wrote that 'self-acting mules have long been a desideratum in the trade and have occupied the attention of intelligent managers and mechanics for some years past; [but] although several have been invented and secured by patent yet none seem to be possessed of sufficient merit to cause any excitement in the trade; in fact they seem so unimportant as to be seldom spoken of'. Eight years later he was producing detailed calculations to show that automatic mules were 15 per cent cheaper to operate than hand mules. Meanwhile, Dr Andrew Ure was publicising a new type of mill designed specifically for automatic mules by William Fairbairn, who was reaching the peak of his career as a Manchester millwright.[8] In 1822 the representative size of the Manchester cotton mill was still 100 to 200 hands, and in the satellite towns it was probably even smaller. This impression was confirmed in another technical work, where a representative factory unit whose costs were 'all calculated from the cost and expense of establishments that have been lately erected' was only a little larger than the

Arkwright prototype, though it contained 4500 spindles and 128 power looms and cost just over £8000. The new mills, by contrast, contained 40,000 spindles and cost over £80,000 – an increase of ten times the capacity of the familiar scale of production. For over fifty years mules had been operated by highly skilled and semi-independent artisans on standard piece-rates, and there was no particular economy in concentration of their numbers; experience showed that the optimum production was reached with 264–288 spindles. But the perfection of Roberts's work enabled one man, with the help of two or three boys, to work 1600 spindles as easily as he had previously worked 300, and mills were doubled in width to accommodate the much enlarged machines [186, *76–81*]. These details may try the patience of those who lack interest in technical problems, but a basic appreciation of the scale and timing of technical change is essential for adequate understanding of such problems as the structure of enterprise and of industry, of capital formation and of labour relations, that follow.

According to the research of von Tunzelmann, there was no perceptible fall in the cost of power used by cotton manufacturers from the 1790s to the mid 1830s, and possibly for another decade after that. Meanwhile, the prices of cotton yarns and fabrics continued to decline, by the 1830s producing unacceptably thin profit margins in the industry. Mill owners looked for ways of reducing costs, economising wherever possible, running machinery and engines faster, integrating spinning and weaving plants, and finally adopting the more efficient type of steam engine whose use had been pioneered in the Cornwall mining industry. Tunzelmann believes that the high cost of power delayed the diffusion of more automated machinery, and there was unquestionably a hiatus in the growth of scale in the 1830s and 1840s. In later chapters it will be seen that there were other factors, notably finance, markets and skilled labour, restraining further evolution of scale until after mid-century [16: *212–24*; 2: 313–18].

3   Capital and Structure of the Industry

A GLANCE at the bibliography will confirm that there has been more academic interest in the amount of capital invested in firms in the cotton industry than in any other aspect of its long history. There are two reasons for this. The original one is that historians have for long been fascinated by the notion most clearly formulated in Samuel Smiles' *Self-Help* (1860), that enterprise was open to men of limited capital who had the character to exploit the opportunities open to them. More recent interest derives from strong interest in development economics, that is, in the conditions necessary for industrialisation, including the initial investment costs. Both topics are evidently much wider than the cotton industry but have focused on it because of the major role played by cotton in the first Industrial Revolution, i.e. in the Industrial Revolution in Britain.

Modern studies have featured growing scepticism about the ability of men of 'humble birth' to become entrepreneurs. Harold Perkin's *Origins of Modern English Society* (1969) scorns the idea as a myth, 'one of the most powerful instruments of propaganda ever developed by any class to justify itself and seduce others to its own ideal' (p. 225), while Katrina Honeyman's *Origins of Enterprise* (1982), which includes an analysis of the origins of Arkwright-type mills and of Bolton and Oldham mule spinning workshops, concludes that restrictions on upward mobility remained as insuperable as they always had been (p. 170). However, a more recent analysis by the French Professor François Crouzet entitled *The First Industrialists* (1985) discerns that while neither the upper class nor the lower orders made a large contribution to the recruitment of industrialists, there was a good deal of upward social mobility in the middle ranks of society (p. 141). To explain this mobility we shall need to look at the capital needs of the entrepreneurs in the cotton industry, while the total capital invested in the industry will aid our understanding of the take-off process.

In the last chapter it was explained that the early technology of the British cotton industry was essentially simple, and most of the mills were on a very small scale compared with developments later in the nineteenth century. Now we must look at the problem of costs, examining the fixed and working capital needs of the early mills and printworks. A few firms owned more than one works, and were sometimes involved in a variety of related activities (merchanting, banking, machine building, etc.) and we shall survey what is known of these forms of capitalism.

Practically all studies of the early factory system in the cotton industry begin with Patrick Colquhoun's pioneer census of Arkwright-type mills in 1788. Colquhoun noted 143 mills dispersed over 27 counties in England, Scotland and Wales, but his figures were assembled in a great hurry for a parliamentary pressure group and have recently been shown to have been a serious underestimate of the total and distortion of the geographical spread. There were at least 208 mills, with many more in Yorkshire, Cheshire and Derbyshire than was previously realised. The building of mills had nearly all taken place since 1781, when Arkwright's patents were first successfully challenged in the courts. The proliferation of plants was largely due to the fact that most of them were built on a simple pattern which closely followed Arkwright's mills at Cromford, three- or four-storey mills measuring about 30 x 10 yards and intended to drive 1000 spindles with a 10-horse-power water wheel [9: *10–15*]. At first sight surviving examples may appear like a gaunt terrace of eight or ten working-class houses.

The early mills were highly vulnerable to destruction by fire so most of them were insured. Consequently we have a measure of their cost (or at any rate, replacement cost), which was around £3000 for the basic 1000 spindles mill, and £5000 for a unit about twice the size that had already made its appearance in 1788. Synthesising these details, and adding estimates made by Hugh Watts of the Sun Fire Office in 1797 and for the Samuel Crompton census of mule spinning machinery in 1812, it is possible to assemble some estimates of the total amount of capital invested in the spinning sector of the cotton industry in its early years (Table III). The spinning mule, which incorporated some of the best technical features of Hargreaves' and Arkwright's machines, was at first manually operated in small workshops in

Bolton, Stockport, and other centres, and again required little fixed capital [29: *107–10*; 52: *186–96*]. The accumulation of fixed capital was not impressive until after the French Wars (Table IV).

The figures assembled here take on more meaning when compared with some earlier developments. In Britain's traditional woollen industry, fulling mills were typically worth £100 to £200 and collections of workshops for various processes seldom rose above £500. In the silk industry, two or three reeling mills built on the Italian model earlier in the century cost over £5000, but these were clearly quite exceptional, and most silkworks evidently cost much less. In any case the total numbers of silk mills were quite small, just 20 or so built over a 50-year period (1720–70). Similarly, a handful of calico-printing works cost over £5000, but much more commonly cost under £2000, and there were probably not more than 50 before 1775. It was the dramatic growth and dispersion of Arkwright-type mills, as much as the size, that marked them out from earlier developments in the textile industry (25: *451–78*; 27: *475–9*].

The number of firms in the industry was always significantly less than the number of factories, for several leading firms had two or more factories. Peels, the biggest firm in 1795, had twenty-three mills centred on Blackburn, Bury, Bolton, Burton upon Trent and Tamworth; William Douglas and his partners had nine, divided between Pendleton (Manchester), Holywell (North Wales coast), Carlisle and Scotland; and Robinsons of Nottingham, who are regularly mentioned in the textbooks as the first firm to buy a Watt steam engine for a cotton mill, had five mills strung along a stream just to the north of the town. David Dale, lately Arkwright's partner in Scotland, had two large mills with two others being built. The great majority of entrepreneurs in the industry were, however, men of much more limited means, dragging themselves up the economic ladder by their bootstraps.

Although the stresses of the French Wars persuaded some moneyed entrepreneurs to withdraw from the industry, and weeded out many of the struggling small men, the structure of the industry continued to be polarised, that is, characterised by a few giants and many small men dependent on the credit of merchants or merchant-manufacturers. By 1812, when the next survey of the industry was taken, mule spinning had easily overtaken roller

Table III Estimates of the Number of and Fixed Capital Invested in British Cotton-spinning Mills, 1787–1812

Estimate	Date	Number of Arkwright-type factories	Number of mule factories and workshops	Value of an Arkwright mill	Adjustment for mule factories	Total fixed capital (£m)	Revised total (£m)
Colquhoun	1787	208	n.d.	£5,000	+£285,000	1.0	1.3
Chapman	1795	c.300	n.d.	£3–5,000	+£500,000	2.0	2.0
Watts	1797	—900—		£3,000	–£200,000	2.7	2.5
Crompton	1812	n.d.	673	n.d.	(none)	3.0–4.0	5.0–6.0

Sources: [18: 235–66; 9: 5–27].

Table IV Estimates of Fixed and Working Capital in the British Cotton Industry, 1834–56

		Spinning and Weaving				
Estimate	Date	Fixed capital (£m)	Working capital (£m)	Total (£m)	Finishing trades (£m)	Total capital (£m)
McCulloch	1834	14.8	7.4	22.2	11.8	34.0
Baynes	1856	31.0	14.5	45.5	30.0	75.5

Source: [17: 358–81].

spinning in importance, but this did not terminate the business careers of all the old leaders. When M'Connel & Kennedy showed the successful application of Watt's steam engine to the 'heavy' motions of the mule, the giants of the industry began to switch their capital to the new system. In 1812, 70 per cent (or 472 out of 673) of the firms in mule spinning had fewer than 10,000 spindles, but a few firms had many times this number: Samuel Horrocks of Preston had 107,000 in eight mills, while Peter Marsland of Stockport, M'Connel and Kennedy, and A and G Murray of Manchester, each had over 80,000, to mention only the leaders. The first two were second-generation firms that had pioneered the industry, the second two machine builders who had begun in the early 1790s with very little capital [29: *107–10*]. The leaders of 1795 had disappeared from the top of the table, but this is partly explained by the limitations of the 1812 census, which did not count the Arkwright-type mills unless they were also used for mule spinning, and extended to only sixty miles around Manchester. Big firms like the Strutts, Arkwrights, Oldknow and Peels at Tamworth and Burton upon Trent, the Douglasses at Holywell, were thus excluded by definition. Evidence to a Parliamentary Committee in 1815–16 adds some details on the size of the workforce in some of the best-known concerns. Robert Owen, the successor to David Dale at New Lanark, was employing 1600–1700, James Finlay and Co 1529 at three mills in Scotland, the Strutts, 1494 at Belper (near Derby), A and G Murray 1215 and M'Connel and Kennedy 1020 [27: *475–9*]. Nevertheless, small entrepreneurs continued to make their way into the industry, especially in the early 1820s.[9]

Useful data on the changing structure of the cotton industry for the period 1815–41 exist in the Manchester rate books and a Factory Inspector's survey of the latter year. The different sources are identified here because they may help to explain differences in the conclusions of scholars who have extracted and analysed the figures. R. Lloyd-Jones, concentrating on the Manchester material, emphasises the high mortality of small firms, and particularly *new* small firms. He maintains that the more successful firms were generally those launched as middle-sized enterprises [33: *72–82*]. V. A. C. Gatrell, concentrating on the 1841 material, prefers to speak of the industry as consisting predominantly of 'small-to-middling sized' firms, and after considering a larger group of firms than that available to Lloyds-Jones for study, concluded that 'the difference between the vulnerability of small firms as against mixed, was surprisingly slight' [20: *121*].

The common ground between these two writers is that, even by the more modest standards of the early nineteenth century, the cotton industry was never dominated by the handful of big capitalists, and it is wrong to write (as Engels did in 1844) of 'ever-increasing concentration of capital in fewer and fewer hands'. The interesting question is to ask the reasons for the apparent failure of big capitalists to dominate the second- and third-generation leadership as Arkwright, Peel, Horrocks, Oldknow and others had the first. Several answers have been offered. D. A. Farnie, taking the long view (1815–96), notices that the combined spinning and weaving firm first appeared in numbers in the 1830s but failed to proliferate due to geographical separation and specialisation, spinning in south Lancashire and the Stockport area, weaving in the north of the county [2: *313–18*]. Gatrell, after querying the existence of substantial economies of scale in the early cotton mills, finds an answer in 'social constraints', a sense of 'moderation in enterprise' among contemporary entrepreneurs (20: *117*]. This obtains some support from the most recent research on cotton mill technology, that referred to at the end of last chapter, which suggests that a further leap forward in the optimum scale of production was delayed until the mid 1840s. However, that would not have dissuaded ambitious entrepreneurs from acquiring several mills.

A further answer is suggested by various authors who have drawn attention to the financial restraints in the growth of firms in the early cotton industry. For most of the period covered by the present study, the provincial money market was evolving from very elementary beginnings, and entrepreneurs in need of capital drew on very diverse sources. The favourite source of capital was retained profits, and during the restricted growth period of Arkwright's patents (1769–85) profit rates are known to have been very high; Robinsons of Nottingham, to take just one example, were earning 100 per cent on their investment in mills and plant in 1784.[10] Even so, working capital requirements were so much larger than fixed capital, and the time-lag between decisions to build and profits so long, that financial difficulties could be experienced. 'I have been with Mr Robinson and he says . . .

building etc. hath swallowed so much money that at present he sells [only] for ready cash', Thomas Oldknow wrote to his brother Samuel at Stockport in 1783 [48: *13*]. Similarly, the first Sir Robert Peel said that in the early part of his career 'the greatest difficulty which he had to surmount was the want of capital to keep pace with his schemes of extension. The profits of the business were exceedingly great, and it admitted of great extension, but for some time the firm were hampered by the limited amount of their capital and credit' [43: *70*]. The correspondence of M'Connel & Kennedy, the Manchester leaders of the fine cotton-spinning industry, makes constant reference in the critical periods of the war years to the difficulties of raising money and to the reluctance of bankers to discount bills [52: *221*]. If the leaders of the industry suffered from intermittent financial strain, it cannot be expected that those who entered the industry after the years of abnormal profits, or who began with fewer connections, were insulated from such difficulties, and several other studies illustrate the financial problems of a variety of firms [40: *171–87*; 39, *32ff*].

Small firms that could not feed their own growth usually turned to their own families, and then to local business and social contracts for help, but of course not all had such connections. The law did not recognise shareholding in the modern sense until the Limited Liability Acts of 1855–6, but from the early part of the eighteenth century it became common for small businesses to borrow money on bond, and widows, clergymen, trustees, executors, retired tradesmen and other people with small savings were often glad to take advantage of this security. Small manufacturers might draw on the resources of a handful of local people who knew and trusted them, but this source of capital was not unfamiliar to much larger concerns. Cardwell, Birley & Hornby, the Blackburn cotton spinners, had ninety-seven small investors on their books in 1812, with a total investment of £36,000. In this instance, nearly all the loans were secured by a simple promise to pay, probably because the lenders were local people known personally to the partners [52: *255–7*]. In Scotland the legal framework was different; six, eight or ten partners in manufacturing concerns was already an established practice at the middle of the eighteenth century, and there was not the same need to draw on external sources.

However, sleeping partners were not uncommon in the English cotton industry, despite the risk of unlimited liability for the debts of the firm. Merchants were sometimes willing to enter into partnership with cotton manufacturers. A good example is provided by Gardom, Pares & Co. of Calver Bridge, near Sheffield, the partners in which consisted of representatives of the Heygate family, London hosiers and bankers, the Pares family, Leicester merchant hosiers, and the Gardoms, a line of Derbyshire hosiers that had become licensees of Arkwright in 1778 [64: *26–8*].

Retired manufacturers would sometimes offer partnerships to promising young men, and a range of speculators entered the trade on similar terms, not infrequently to their loss. Improving landlords were often willing to provide or improve buildings for their tenantry, so that the cotton industry in Manchester and other parts of Lancashire owes something to the self-interest of the Earls of Derby, that of Glossop to the Duke of Norfolk, the Colne valley to Lord Dartmouth, and the Mansfield area (Notts.) to the Duke of Portland. In Glasgow the trading elite were intermarrying with the leading landowning families in Scotland in the second half of the eighteenth century, and partnerships to develop and exploit the best water-power sites in the country areas were common. Manufacturers fortunate enough to own land or buildings could readily mortgage them to raise capital or convert them to new uses [52: *195–8*].

Other channels might be open to entrepreneurs who were seeking working capital. A variety of historical business records show that widespread encouragement was given to small manufacturers by the supplier merchants' habit of allowing four to eight months' credit, a sufficient period to work up the raw material and sell the product to wholesalers who, in some cases, might make payments in cash or bills of exchange [52: *225–30*]. The difficulty with such records is that they may not be representative; certainly they are likely to neglect the kind of small entrepreneur whose pocket-book records have seldom survived. The early development of mercantile credit was certainly a factor in the growth of the cotton industry, but many of those who became manufacturers were men of little education and few connections, and lived from hand to mouth. Authentic spokesmen from their ranks are difficult to find, but there is an occasional voice. Thus John Dugdale of the Lowerhouse Print Works, near Burnley, made some remarks in 1847 which, when translated from the vernacular, read: 'If you'll look back for the last six years, you'll find half of the printers are broken [bankrupt], and half of those that are left cannot break, for nobody will trust them; and the rest get on as well as they can.' A firm-by-firm survey of the Lancashire calico printers in 1846 confirms the impression of a preponderance of small and struggling entrepreneurs, with a high turnover of firms [4: 70–3].

London merchants and wholesale dealers also provided credit for northern manufacturers, but experience taught them to be highly selective. The spectacular bankruptcy in 1788 of Livesey, Hargreaves & Co. of Blackburn, the leading calico printers in the trade, was a severe setback to a number of London bankers. Samuel Oldknow, the early leader of the English muslin industry, was refused £5000 credit by Saltes, his main London customers, in 1790 [48: 148; 43: 28–33]. John Watson & Sons, the leading Preston cotton manufacturers, were more persuasive with their London customers, and at the time of their failure in 1809 had over £10,000 in credit from them[11]. These examples, and others which can be extracted from the records of the court of bankruptcy, show that the granting of credit was a risky business, even with the leading firms.

However, it seems that the most significant cause of stunted growth was the immaturity of the capital markets in the textile regions of the north of England. The early country banks were small family enterprises whose partners were characteristically inexperienced in banking and unprepared to meet the unprecedented developments in industry and overseas markets. Bank failures were frequent and prudent manufacturers often felt it wisest to avoid all banks. After 1826 the Bank of England lost its monopoly of joint-stock banking in the industrial districts, and the capital held by the private banks was quickly superseded by that of new local joint-stock banks. However, the new banks, governed by part-time directors, often proved even more erratic in their business than the older private banks, and after the financial crisis of 1836–7 the survivors were forced to resort to the most conservative policies, granting credit on only the strongest security and avoiding risk wherever possible. The period following the French Wars also saw the rise of what are now known as merchant banks, originally leading merchants of London, Glasgow and Liverpool who accepted (i.e. guaranteed payment of) bills of exchange, usually for foreign trade, but financial crises also compelled these firms to pursue conservative policies [19; 22]. The problem of recruiting adequate working capital continued as a serious restraint on the growth of cotton manufacturers until incorporation of firms became common towards the end of the century.

4   Commercial Organisation and Markets

ALL the raw material used in the cotton industry was imported, and an organisation had to be evolved to supply the manufacturers with increasing quantities of raw cotton (or cotton wool, as it was generally known). From the early 1780s merchants and manufacturers recognised that further growth depended on increased supplies of cotton at low prices, particularly the finer qualities, and they were not slow to press their views with the Board of Trade and the planters. However, projects to increase the cotton crop in the West Indies (especially the Bahamas) and introduce the commodity into Sierra Leone met with only a limited response. The East India Company was reluctant to export the finer Indian staples as it was anxious to maintain its trade in Indian muslins, which depended on a restricted supply. The most encouraging response at first came from Brazil, where the crop was encouraged by the Portuguese government, but this source was quickly superseded in the 1790s by the rapid expansion of cotton in the southern plantations of the recently established United States of America. In the early 1790s the profits on the cotton crop were high, and quickly displaced other cash crops, such as rice, indigo and tobacco. The supply of land seemed almost unlimited, particularly after the Louisiana purchase of 1801, and the United States cotton crop rose from 2 million lb in 1791 to 182 million lb in 1821, becoming the major source of Lancashire's supply at the turn of the century. The high elasticity of supply of cotton, due primarily to the responsiveness of the American planters and the adoption of Whitney's cotton gin, was clearly a crucial factor in the phenomenal growth of the British cotton industry in these years [52: *Ch. 5*].

The American planters were so successful in increasing the productivity of the cotton plantations, and the marketing machinery improved to such an extent, that after 1800 prices embarked on a course of more or less continuous decline. The

United States Government's attempts to impose restrictions on exports in the period from December 1807 to May 1810 caused erratic fluctuations in prices at Liverpool, but did not affect the long-term trend. The elements of cost in the price of yarn can be illustrated from the data shown in Table V. During the period of the French Wars, when it became more difficult to import wool from the Continent to supply the West Riding and other English manufacturers, the price of wool rose steeply, bringing an unexpected bonus to the cotton industry, and offering a further incentive to woollen and worsted manufacturers and merchants to turn over to cotton. The best price data available can give little conception of the lament of England's old staple industry. As early as 1802 Robert Davison, a Nottingham hosier and spinner, complained that 'the high price of wool has produced a very great and alarming rivalry in cotton fabrics . . . the substitution of the latter for the former is immense . . . large mills and factories originally destined to the working of woollens have been compelled to devote their works to cotton' [26: *215*]. In the West Riding, the displacement of worsteds by calicoes was at first amply compensated for by the rise of carpet making, upholstery, coach linings and other new branches, but by 1808 the Manchester trade dominated the Halifax and Colne areas and the upper Calder valley. The outcome was that the woollen and worsted

Table V Elements of Cost in the Price of Yarn, 1779–1812

Yarn 40 hanks to the lb (roller spun)

	1779	1784	1799	1812
Selling price	16s. 0d.	10s. 11d.	7s. 6d.	2s. 6d.
Cost of cotton	2s. 0d.	2s. 0d.	3s. 4d.	1s. 6d.
Labour and capital	14s. 0d.	8s. 11d.	4s. 2d.	1s. 0d.

Yarn 100 hanks to the lb (mule spun)

	1786	1796	1806	1812
Selling price	38s. 0d.	19s. 0d.	7s. 2d.	5s. 2d.
Cost of cotton	4s. 0d.	3s. 6d.	3s. 0d.	2s. 4d.
Labour and capital	34s. 0d.	15s. 6d.	4s. 2d.	2s. 10d.

Source: T. Ellison, *The Cotton Trade of Great Britain* (1886) p. 55; see [53: *75–83*].

industry, and not least the older centres in the West Country and East Anglia, suffered more reverses during the French Wars than did cotton.[12]

The organisation that evolved to market the cotton wool, the spun cotton yarns and cotton cloth was a complex one, and we can deal only with its salient features here. The need for numerous specialised functions can be readily appreciated from features of the industry that have already been noticed: the preponderance of small manufacturers, rapidly changing technology, considerable day-by-day fluctuations in market prices (sometimes due to war or commercial crisis, sometimes to capricious movements in fashion, and occasionally to unfounded rumour), and fairly widespread and regular shortages of capital. To these factors must be added slow and expensive communications, especially to the American, Indian and other distant markets, and the fact that the structure of commerce was slowly evolving for most of our period, certainly from 1780 to 1830. Much of what follows in the remainder of this section illustrates these features.

London was the principal port for cotton until at least 1795, and after that time London merchants and their agents were active in Liverpool, Manchester and other northern centres. Towards the end of the century Liverpool rivalled London because most of the mills and workshops in the cotton industry were situated within sixty or eighty miles of the port, and had good canal and river connections with it. The rise of the United States as the major supplier of raw cotton was also an important factor. The cotton planter was separated from the mill owner by a range of specialised intermediaries; some big manufacturers tried to by-pass the system and deal directly with the growers, but commitment to any one source was found to be an unwise policy. The cotton wool was imported by ship-owning merchants or commission agents acting for the planter or exporter, often a British merchant resident in the United States. In the late eighteenth century the bags of imported cotton were brought up and distributed by Manchester cotton dealers, but these men were gradually superseded by the Liverpool cotton brokers, particularly after the opening of the Liverpool and Manchester railway (1830). Some of the brokers were offshoots of Liverpool merchant houses, but most of them migrated to the port from Manchester and the manufacturing districts. The successful broker combined knowledge of the needs of the industry (derived from his early experience in the mills and regular contacts with buyers) with daily intimacy with the cotton market and a reputation for 'strict probity and honour'. He needed capital, though many began their careers at Liverpool with slender financial resources. The fifty Manchester cotton dealers mentioned in a local directory of 1804 had been replaced by some ninety firms of Liverpool brokers in 1841, the year the Cotton Brokers' Association was formed. The cotton market at Liverpool was a highly competitive one, approximating to the economist's definition of a 'perfect market'. By constant circulation of samples and information bulletins (known as 'cotton circulars'), the brokers provided the 'perfect knowledge' necessary for the maintenance of this market [52: *Ch. 6*; 53: *75–83*].

As the cotton trade expanded and became more sophisticated in its organisation and finance, the Liverpool family firms who had provided the enterprise for the eighteenth-century development of the port were augmented by branches of merchant houses from the United States, London and Glasgow. The number of merchants importing cotton into Liverpool in any one year ran into hundreds, but a large proportion of the trade was handled by a small group of some thirty operators who specialised in the import of cotton, mostly from the United States alone [56: *182–211*].

In discussing the structure of the industry, we have already examined the trend towards disintegration that set in at an early stage of expansion. Vertically integrated firms like Peels, Arkwrights and Douglases were exceptional even in their day, and their relative importance appears to have declined. The existence of a large number of small firms specialising in carding and spinning gave rise to another specialised market, that for yarns. The larger spinners, like Strutts of Belper and M'Connel & Kennedy of Manchester, had selling agents in all the markets – Glasgow, Belfast, Nottingham and other centres – constantly instructing them on prices for the different yarn counts. The smaller spinners were usually dependent on yarn merchants or brokers, who allowed them cotton wool on credit and bought up their small consignments. Here, as elsewhere, the market was a highly competitive one, and those with little capital depended on the favour of merchants and were most vulnerable to sudden changes in demand [46: *Ch. 5*; 44: *Ch. 11*; 52: *Ch. 7*].

Between 1780 and 1815 the market for cotton cloth continued to be centred on London, but that period saw a decisive shift of the focus of trade towards Manchester. Though a few outstanding northern firms like the Peels of Manchester and I. & R. Morley, the Nottingham hosiers, opened their own warehouses in London before the end of the century, the London tradesmen's more ready access to capital and their close contact with fashion movements contrived to tie provincial merchants and manufacturers to them. There appear to have been three common types of connection between the centre of trade and the centres of manufacturing. Some firms in the provinces had a partner in London or a working agreement with a London merchant, and this close personal connection was particularly important in fashion lines like calico printing and hosiery. Other goods from the provinces were handled by commission agents who sold by private contract or at weekly public sales, or by warehousemen who bought goods outright from the provincial manufacturers. Unwin's *Samuel Oldknow and the Arkwrights* provides some fascinating insights into the ways a London buyer could advise a manufacturer on market requirements and encourage him to improve his product, take up new lines and drop more traditional ones.

The emergence of Manchester as the international emporium for cotton goods can be traced to a number of developments around the turn of the century. The necessity for keeping a warehouse or stockroom in Manchester soon spread beyond the Lancashire manufacturing region. In the 1790s Midlands and West Riding cotton spinners were maintaining stocks for sale in the town, and the Scots soon learned that it saved time to meet drapers there rather than travel the country towns for small orders. London warehousemen found it an advantage to keep an agent posted at the centre of manufacturing. A growing concourse of country drapers was drawn to the street markets and inns to scramble for bargains, or to jostle at the counters of the ever-increasing numbers of warehouses. Some idea of the rapidity of growth of trade is indicated by the number of warehouses in the town, which leaped from 120 in 1772 to 729 in 1815 and 955 in 1829, though many of these would be converted tenements in the original warehouse district in and around Cannon Street and High Street [52: *172–4*; 35: *80*].

In the train of provincial manufacturers and London warehousemen came overseas merchants. The technical advances of the later eighteenth century were quickly sought out by the French government, who soon had English artisans working in their country. 'You can keep a secret in a German factory, because the workers are obedient, prudent, and satisfied with a little; but the English workers are insolent, quarrelsome, adventurous and greedy for money. It is never difficult to seduce them from their employment', the French minister Calonne declared in 1788. Scattered accounts of the careers of English artisans who went abroad suggest that several showed similar personality traits in their dealings with European firms and governments and not infrequently cost their hosts much expense and trouble with little benefit. The French Revolution and the French Wars dislocated trade severely, and hampered the illegal migration of men and machinery across the Channel, so that it was not until the 1830s that French and Belgian textile technology showed signs of catching up with the British, while the Germans and other Continental countries were even further behind. One consequence was that increasing numbers of German, Dutch, Swiss, French and Italian merchants were drawn to Manchester, and after 1835 they were followed by Greeks, Spaniards, Portuguese, Russians and other traders [3: 25; 49: 99–115; 50: 10–48].

The presence of this large colony of Continental merchants in Manchester must not be taken as indicative of British merchants' lack of interest in the export market. We have already noticed the existence of a vigorous export trade to Africa, America and France at the middle of the eighteenth century. There is, however, evidence to suggest that the dramatic growth of industrial production in the Industrial Revolution period severely strained the existing commercial organisation and led, after an interval, to new organisation of overseas marketing.

For most of the eighteenth century, London merchant enterprise maintained its traditional leadership, reinforced by the immigration of branches of wealthy houses from the Continent and from the English provinces. The period from about 1770 to the end of the French Wars saw the first vigorous generation of provincial manufacturers taking initiatives in marketing, often beginning with connections in the US and sometimes backed by the financial resources of well-established mercantile houses in London, Amsterdam, or one of the other Continental centres. This can be seen as part of a wider process of the extension of entrepreneurs' functions on the 'new frontiers' of British industrial expansion. However, a large turnover of firms (especially during the difficult trading conditions of the French Wars), heavy losses in some new markets (especially Latin America), and the emergence of specialisation within the industrialising regions, soon reduced this bold initiative to small proportions. The business of exporting was taken over, in the first quarter of the century, by a new three-tier structure consisting of provincial manufacturers, overseas commission merchants, and leading London merchants (soon to be called merchant banks or accepting houses). The latter took the financial strain by lending their names to ('accepting') the bills of exchange that were general means of payment in international trade.[13]

The system worked tolerably well during the periods of growth but was liable to grind to a halt during the recurrent periods of commercial crisis (1788, 1797, 1808, 1825, 1836−7, 1847−8 . . .) that hit the British and international economies. At these times, a train of bankruptcies at home and abroad evaporated confidence so quickly that it became nearly impossible for the most creditworthy manufacturers and commission houses to obtain the credit they needed, while similar firms and those with their profits invested in unsalable land or property often went to the wall. Manufacturers and merchants selling in the more distant markets, such as India, China and South America, were particularly vulnerable to sudden shifts in confidence in the financial markets. They were moreover unusually exposed to risks from ignorance of varying fashions in such distant places due to the long months in which letters and cargoes were in transit. The struggles of firms that tried to make their living in these markets make fascinating reading; a handful made fortunes and established dynasties, but most did not last a generation.

Nevertheless the overseas demand for British cottons grew dramatically. The figures recalculated by the late Ralph Davis (Tables VI and VII) make earlier estimates obsolete. From the mid 1780s to the mid 1840s, cottons came to account for something approaching half of all British exports (Table VI). Until the end of the eighteenth century, practically all the exports went to Continental Europe, North America and the West Indies, though some of the gains were at the expense of Britain's traditional export of woollen cloth. Exports to these 'old' markets continued to

42

Table VI Total British Exports and Exports of British Cottons 1784–1856 (£m)

	1784–6	1794–6	1804–6	1814–16	1824–6	1834–6	1844–6	1854–6
Total	12.7	21.8	37.5	44.4	35.3	46.2	58.4	102.5
Cotton	0.8	3.4	15.9	18.7	16.9	22.4	25.8	34.9
(%)	6.0	15.6	42.3	42.1	47.8	48.5	44.2	34.1

Source: adapted from [51: 15].

Table VII Export of Cotton Goods to 'Old' and 'New' Markets 1784–1856 (£m)

	'Old markets'	'New markets'	Total	New as % of total
1784–6	0.8	0	0.8	0
1794–6	3.4	0	3.4	0
1804–6	15.2	0.7	15.9	4.4
1814–16	17.0	1.7	18.7	9.1
1824–6	12.3	4.5	16.9	26.6
1834–6	15.0	7.4	22.4	33.0
1844–6	13.2	12.6	25.8	48.8
1854–6	16.0	19.0	34.9	54.4

Source: calculated from [51: 21].

increase in the first half of the century, but as a proportion of total exports they fell quite sharply. The introduction of the American tariff in 1815 and the removal of British restrictions on the export of machinery in 1843 are well-known bench marks in this shift, but industrialisation of the more advanced countries was the underlying cause. By contrast, the share of new markets in Latin America and the Orient showed astonishing growth, with British India taking the largest share (Table VII). This trend was accompanied by an overall deterioration in the quality of cotton fabrics produced so as to meet the needs of consumers in poorer countries.

5 Labour and Industrial Relations

IN approaching the problems of recruitment of labour and of industrial relations, it is convenient to make an initial distinction between factory and domestic labour. Increasing quantities of cotton goods at falling prices were responsible for increases in the numbers of men, women and juveniles employed in both categories for most of the period covered by this study, but in almost all other respects the characteristics of the labour force in the two sectors were quite different. They must therefore be considered separately, while recognising the important links between them.

The main problem in recruiting a factory labour force was the reluctance of workers to enter the mills, particularly in the country areas where even large workshops were unfamiliar. Arkwright had no difficulty in filling his Manchester mill in 1783 – indeed he had so many applications that he had to turn good families away – but eight miles away, at Styal, the Gregs had to scrape together a labour force from the country round about and from more distant workhouses [66: *14*]. Similar contrasts can be drawn between the experience of mill owners in Nottingham and Glasgow and those in the respective country areas [26: *164–8*; 40: *188–95*], with the proviso that the first major factory enterprise in the smaller towns might soak up the entire available labour supply. When Charles Hulbert opened a cotton mill at Shrewsbury in 1803, he found that his main difficulty was to recruit a labour force, because 'the great linen mills of Messrs Marshall, Benyon and Bage had taken the lead and the great portion of young people willing to be employed in manufactories were engaged'. Moreover, Hulbert explained, young people in agricultural areas (where the mill owners were forced to resort for water power) were slower to learn, and 'many of our instructed workpeople, notwithstanding all were engaged at regular wages for three years, left us for Manchester, Stockport, etc. . . . . We

45

soon found that if business must be carried on to any great extent where hand labour was required, it must be in the neighbourhood of like manufactories, where an advance of wages would speedily obtain the number of hands required.'[14]

The mill owners' problem can only be understood by examining the recruitment of skilled workers (machine builders, millwrights and mule spinners) separately from that of the unskilled machine minders who formed the majority of the labour force in Arkwright-type mills. The fundamental difficulty in obtaining skilled men was simply the consequence of the rapid growth of the cotton industry, which made artisans with relevant skills very much at a premium. Local newspaper advertisements, memoirs, private correspondence and high wage rates all bear testimony to the acute shortage of craftsmen whose skills could be applied to textile machine building or to the installation of water wheels and transmission systems.

The aversion of unskilled labour to employment in cotton mills largely stemmed from dislike of long, uninterrupted shifts in the mill (agricultural and domestic labour was generally more intermittent), and from the similarity of the early factories to the parish workhouses. The comparison often made between the two was not so much a question of architecture, or of the stigma attached to workhouse labour, so much as the insistence in both on close and continuous supervision of work by overseers. The consequence of this popular repugnance to factory life was that employment in the mills often represented casual labour for those who, for the time being, could find nothing better, and as late as the 1830s Samuel Greg regarded the 'restless and migratory spirit' of his mill workers as one of the main problems which troubled him as an employer.[15]

The literature on labour in the early factory system is very largely an examination of the techniques that were used to recruit and retain a workforce, and the varying responses to them. The obvious solution, as Hulbert concluded, was to offer better wage rates than one's competitors, and factory wages quickly rose above those offered to agricultural labourers and to workers in domestic industry; by 1834 it was claimed (without contradiction) that 'The wages in the cotton factories of Lancashire are the best in England', while 'the poor's rate is lower than in any other manufacturing district' [66: 47, n. 3]. However, experience soon showed that big wage packets were not the only solution, particularly where it was necessary to attract workers to isolated mill sites. At Cromford, Arkwright found it necessary to offer employment to whole families, and to build houses before they could be induced to move from Nottingham, Derby or Manchester. By 1790 he was providing a public house, a weekly market and garden allotments to retain his workforce [44: *246–60*]. The Strutts at Belper, David Dale at New Lanark, the Evanses at Darley Abbey, the Gregs at Styal, and other factory colony builders had to offer comparable incentives, but, like Arkwright, they found that the establishment of a new community was an expensive and often frustrating experience, and labour turnover continued at a very high rate [40: *188–95*; 69: *277–301*; 66: *39–43*].

The remoter mills were unable to collect a labour force even by advertising, and had to have recourse to the workhouse for their unskilled workers. The late eighteenth century was a period of rapid population growth, and many of the workhouses of London and the southern counties were glad to send consignments of pauper children to the northern mills for an apprenticeship of anything from a year to eight years, depending on their age. The pauper apprenticeship system has often been discussed in terms of exploitation of juvenile labour, and there can be no doubt that the children worked long hours for abysmal wages. But the few records of the system that have survived show that the apprenticeship system was not as cheap as free labour. It was in any case short-lived, partly because as the first generation of apprentices grew to adulthood the colony became self-perpetuating, but more especially because after the turn of the century the Arkwright-type mills were giving way to mule spinning factories, for which the availability of water power was a less important factor in location [26: *169–71*; 66: *45*].

Having collected and housed his labour force, the factory master's problems were by no means over. He had to train his machine operatives and, what was much more difficult, to induce them to become willing, obedient, regular, punctual and sober servants of his company. The most successful entrepreneurs of the Industrial Revolution were those who succeeded in imposing their system of work discipline on their labour force, and the cotton industry nurtured two or three of the outstanding figures in this small group of men of iron determination. Arkwright, according to the earliest informed account of his activities, introduced into every department of the cotton manufacture 'a system of industry, order and cleanliness, till then unknown in any manufactory where great numbers were employed together, but which he so effectually accomplished that his example may be regarded as the origin of almost all similar improvement'.[16] Like Arkwright, the first Sir Robert Peel 'introduced among his operatives that order, arrangement and sub-division of employment which form the marked characteristics of the factory system . . . he insisted on a system of punctuality and regularity which approached the discipline of military drill' [43: 56].

Pollard has analysed the methods that were used to institute and maintain this new regimen.[17] The most common deterrents were corporal punishment (for juveniles), fines for breaking the factory rules, and the threat of dismissal. However, the history of industrial relations in the industry shows that workers were not always easily intimidated, and James Montgomery's *Carding and Spinning Master's Assistant* (1832) advised that 'operatives are generally unwilling to submit to fines either for bad work or improper conduct; it seems to be a general feeling amongst them that they would much rather have the master turn them away than fine them'. Incentives, notably some system of payment by results, were also widely used. The third method, comprehensible only in the light of the employers' need to establish a novel pattern of work on a large scale, was the attempt to inculcate in the workers the mill owners' own set of values and priorities. The ultimate aspiration of the mill owner for his workpeople can be seen in the Strutts' boast of their success in bringing sober and industrious habits to Belper. The manufacturing squires at factory colonies like Belper had virtual control of the whole of the local population, but their authority must not be exaggerated. Boyson's recent study of the Ashworths of Turton (a factory colony near Bolton) portrays two brothers with a messianic sense of the cotton manufacturers' destiny as the nation's spirit of enterprise and social conscience, but adds that their employees 'accepted the social and moral standards set by the Ashworths, but politically their views were their own' [39: *135*].

The early nineteenth-century literature on the cotton industry has distorted our view of the industry by giving undue prominence to the factory colonies; influential work like J. P. Kay's *Condition of the Working Classes employed in the Cotton Manufacture in Manchester*

48

(1832) and W. Cooke Taylor's *Notes of a Tour in the Manufacturing Districts of Lancashire* (1841) saw the model factory colony as the ideal arrangement of industrial society. But, as we have already noted, the factory colony had reached its meridian by the turn of the century, and at the end of the French Wars the urban mule spinning mills had become the predominant form of enterprise; Bolton was much more typical of the industry than Belper. Mule spinners have already been mentioned as one of the grades of artisans whose skills were very much at a premium, and their position in the structure of industrial relations must now be examined more closely. Mule spinning, as we saw in Section 2, was only mechanised slowly, and even when the automatic mule became widely adopted (after about 1835), the spinner retained his quasi-independent status. A generation after the period covered by this book, the finest spinning still depended on the sensitive touch of the mule spinner, while spinners of the medium and coarser yarns successfully contrived to introduce individuality to their machines. Catling explains that 'every operative spinner was firmly of the opinion that no two mules could ever be made alike. As a consequence he proceeded to tune and adjust each of his own particular pair of mules with little respect for the intentions of the maker or the principles of engineering. Before very long, no two mules ever were alike . . . [and] it was usually unwise to move a spinner about other than in exceptional circumstances' [7:*118, 149*].

All the available wage statistics confirm that the mule spinner was the best-paid artisan in the cotton industry (apart from overlookers) throughout the period covered by this study [e.g 1: *436,438,442−3*]. In the mill, he enjoyed semi-independent status, was paid on piece-rates, employed his own assistants (one or two 'piecers' for each mule) and owed responsibility only to the spinning room overlooker, who was (with the engineer, the carder and the warehouseman) answerable to the general manager. The accounts of a typical small warp and mule spinning mill of the mid 1830s, employing forty people, show that the four mule spinners and their piecers took half of the weekly wage bill of £24. Outside the mill, his status in the community was recognised by the best rooms in some public houses being marked 'Mule Spinners Only'. The mule spinners maintained their own trade unions, the Manchester one well established in 1795, and those in other centres apparently close to its heels. By 1815 the mule spinners' unions, together with those of the equally elite calico printers, impressed the employers as a 'most formidable' group of militant organisations which they had to reckon with [7: *Chs 9–10*; 43: *95–6*].

In Section 2 we saw that carding and spinning became factory processes some thirty or forty years before weaving, and the consequence was an ever-increasing demand for handloom weavers, many of whom had to be recruited further and further afield from the old centres of the cotton industry. Cardwell, Birley & Hornby, the Blackburn merchants and spinners, increased their weavers from 132 in 1777 to 770 in 1788; at the other extremity of the Lancashire region, William Radcliffe was distributing warps to weavers up to thirty miles from Mellor, on the Pennine side of Stockport. By the end of the century Sir Robert Peel had fifteen depots as far apart as Blackburn in the north, Stockport in the south, Chapel-en-le-Frith (Derbyshire) to the east, and Walton (Liverpool) to the west. Very often the growth points were no more than a mile or two out of town, as surviving loomhouses on the Pennine scarp above Oldham and Rochdale show, but in other instances villages at a distance from the established urban centres were suddenly brought to new prosperity by migrating capital. Burnley, for instance, because a major centre of the cotton industry when several Bolton merchant-manufacturers 'began to employ a great number of weavers and spinners in the cotton branch'. Similarly, the skills of the muslin weavers of Paisley induced Peels, Arkwrights and other Lancashire cotton firms to invest capital in developments there, and so successful was this partnership that when John Marshall (the Leeds flex spinner) visited Scotland in 1803, he maintained that Manchester fine spinning and Paisley production of fine fabrics were the two complementary branches of the cotton industry.[18]

Bythell's important study of *The Handloom Weavers* shows the difficulties of acquiring reliable estimates of the total number of cotton weavers before 1833, but it is possible to calculate the order of magnitude (see Table VIII). In 1811, G. A. Lee and Thomas Ainsworth conducted a census of mule spinning and concluded that it employed 150,000 weavers and was responsible for two-thirds of the output of the industry. The other third obviously came from the sector operating Arkwright's technique and, *pro*

Table VIII   Estimates of the Numbers of Domestic Workers in the Cotton Industry, 1795–1833

	Handloom weavers (cotton only)	Auxiliaries	Framework knitters	
1795	75,000[a]	15,000[b]	1782	20,000[c]
1811	225,000[a]	45,000[b]	1812	29,600[c]
1833	250,000[b]	50,000[b]	1844	48,500[c]

Sources: [a] G. J. French, *The Life and Times of Samuel Crompton* (1859; new edn 1970) pp. 275–8.
[b] D. Bythell, *The Handloom Weavers* (1969) pp. 54–7, 86.
[c] Hosiery statistics most conveniently summarised in D. M. Smith, 'The British Hosiery Industry at the Middle of the Ninteteenth Century', *Transactions of the Institute of British Geographers*, XXXI (1963) 129.

rata, must have found employment for 75,000 weavers, making 225,000 in all. Until the mid 1790s the mule sector was still very small, and after that time the Arkwright sector ceased to grow, so that 75,000 cotton weavers would approach a fair estimate for 1795. These figures are consistent with abundant literary evidence of the rapid growth of handloom weaving from around 1780 to the end of the French Wars. The number of domestic framework knitters also multiplied, but unfortunately there are no statistics to distinguish cotton frames from those engaged on knitting wool, silk and linen. The number of workers in the domestic sector of the cotton industry may be compared with 220,000 employed in nearly 1200 mills in Great Britain and Ireland in 1833 [*1*: *394*]. Clearly, the number of domestic workers exceeded the number of factory workers until at least the mid 1830s, when the power loom won the confidence of the mill owners.

The dispersion of the handloom weavers over a large part of Lancashire and the adjacent parts of Cheshire, Derbyshire and the West Riding, as well as the Glasgow–Paisley area, prevented them from uniting to defend their living standards, and their protracted capitulation to the power loom constitutes one of the most miserable chapters of social history. Inevitably, such pathos has attracted a great deal of writing and a variety of interpretations, often flavoured by the political presuppositions of the contributors to the debate. Most recently, Bythell, and Thompson's *The*

Making of the English Working Class, have offered sharply contrasting explanations of the significance of the downward trend of weavers' incomes after the French Wars. Thompson sees self-employed weavers, yeoman weavers and journeyman weavers all thrust down into the same debased proletariat, while Bythell maintains that by 1815 cotton handloom weaving had largely become an unskilled and casual occupation which provided part-time work for women and children, a reservoir of labour that was accustomed to flow into varying channels with the changing seasons and state of trade. While admitting that 'there was terrible suffering in some districts in the 1820s, 1830s, and early 1840s' (particularly in fringe areas like Burnley, Colne and Padiham, where few new mills were being built or equipped with power looms), Bythell thinks that 'most of the handloom weavers in the cotton industry were absorbed into alternative employment with remarkable speed and ease' [65: 271]. This divergence of views, both depending on incomplete evidence, can only be evaluated when we have the benefit of more local studies, particularly those founded on parish registers and the census enumerators' returns of 1841, 1851 and 1861. In the meantime, the only safe comment that can be made is that the standards of living of workers in the cotton industry, like those in the economy at large, show a bewildering variety of contrasts, not only between occupations, but over periods of time and between different localities.

6 The Role of Cotton in the Growth of the Economy

THE period between about 1450 and 1750 saw relatively few mechanical inventions introduced into the European textile industries; the stocking frame at the end of the sixteenth century and the Dutch loom in the seventeenth appear to be the only conspicuous exceptions to this generalisation. The great burst of invention that began with Arkwright and Crompton has some roots reaching down earlier in the century, but the desultory reception of Kay's flying shuttle and Lewis Paul's roller spinning in the 1730s and 1740s occurred in a different economic climate from the last thirty years of the century. Most of the explanations that are offered on the causes of this unprecedented period of technical development have been familiar to historians for a long time: a chronic shortage of yarn and steeply rising costs as weavers adopting the flying shuttle had to draw their yarn supplies from domestic spinners further and further away; the physical qualities of cotton, which make it peculiarly amenable to mechanical handling; and the high elasticity of supply of raw cotton from the rapidly growing United States.

The growing consumption of cotton must have been initiated by an increase in demand and on this point Eversley provides some help. He postulated that between 1750 and 1780 the number of households in the middle income range (£50 to £400 p.a.) rose from 15 per cent of the population of England to 20 or even 25 per cent. In Eversley's model the foundation of the Industrial Revolution was laid by the sale of articles of everyday life to this 'middle class' of consumers.[19] Cotton fits well into this thesis in the middle decades of the eighteenth century in so far as the widespread and growing sale of linen mixtures and printed goods largely issued from this sector of the population, and formed the basis from which sales of cheaper machine-spun and printed cottons accelerated after about 1780, aided by a shift in fashion.

53

The role of cotton in the British economy in the last two decades of the eighteenth century has been the subject of lively debate following the publication of Rostow's 'take-off' theory of economic growth. Searching for a framework in which to set the evolution of modern industrial societies, he suggested that there were five stages of economic growth: the traditional society, the satisfaction of preconditions for 'take-off', the 'take-off', the drive to maturity, and the age of high mass consumption. In Rostow's words, 'the "take-off" consists, in essence, of the achievement of rapid growth in a limited group of sectors, where modern industrial techniques are applied'. He identified cotton textiles as the leading sector in 'take-off' in Britain, and defined the take-off period as 1783–1802, citing the spectacular increase in the import of raw cotton in the decades 1781–91 (319 per cent) and 1791–1801 (67 per cent) as his empirical support [74, *4–12, 53–4*].

The idea of cotton making the decisive advance that impelled the whole economy forward into rapid industrial growth is evidently a bold one, and provoked critical examinations by a number of economists and historians, particularly by Phyllis Deane and W. A. Cole. They calculated that it is unlikely that cotton contributed more than 5 per cent of the British national income by the end of Rostow's take-off (see Table IX). The figure (assuming for a moment that it is correct) demonstrates that cotton was already making an impressive contribution to the economy. But Habakkuk and Deane also calculated that iron was making an equivalent contribution to the economy at the period, and if their figures are accepted it is difficult to understand how cotton alone can be labelled *the* leading sector [72: *71*].

However, Deane and Cole's estimates of the value of the output of the cotton industry are admitted to be 'highly tentative', and any calculation of its contribution to British national income must be even more hazardous. These calculations depend on a sequence of estimates extracted from the controversial pamphlet literature of the period (see Table IX col. (2)). The best that can be said for them is that they appear to have been synthesised from statistics of the value of retained imports (i.e imports minus re-exports), but (Table IX col. (3)), shows that the different estimators multiplied these figures by anything from 2.0 to 5.3, an inconsistency that hints strongly at the possibility of error. The

Table IX Estimates of the Output of the Cotton Industry and its Contribution to National Income, 1760–1817

Years	(1) Retained imports (£m)	(2) Gross value of output (£m)	(3) Multiplier (2) ÷ (1)	(4) Value added (£m) (2) − (1)	(5) National income (£m)	(6) Value added as % of national income
1760	0.2	0.6	3.0	0.4		
1772–4	0.2	0.9	4.5	0.6		
1781–3	1.0	4.0	4.0	2.0	c. 160	c. 1%
1784–6	1.6	5.4	3.4	3.8		
1787–9	2.3	7.0	3.0	4.7		
1795–7	2.6	10.0	4.0	7.4		
1798–1800	5.7	11.1	2.0	5.4		
1801–3	4.0	15.0	3.7	11.0	230	4–5%
1805–7	4.5	18.9	4.2	14.4		
1811–13	5.3	28.3	5.3	23.0	301	7–8%
1815–17	8.3	30.0	3.7	21.7		

Source: [71: 185, 188]. Table 42 has been simplified and col. (3) inserted by present author (see text).

value of the imported raw material was more than doubled at the spinning stage (see Table V), and one suspects that the estimates used by Deane and Cole neglect value added at the bleaching, dyeing and (above all) printing stages. Peels, the leading printers at the end of the eighteenth century, sold their rolls at £4 to £5 each, but it seems they were worth only £1.30 as white calico [43: 79].

The possible errors in Table IX can be illustrated in another way. Their estimate for 1798–1800 may appear to be an exception to my remarks about the limitations of Deane and Cole's figures for gross output, as it was made by Eden for the Globe Insurance Company. Eden's original figure was £10 million, but the previous year the secretaries of the Sun Fire Office, Royal Exchange and Phoenix insurance companies procured information 'from cotton spinners and from an engineer who has built many mills' and calculated that the value of the output of the industry 'amounts to about £20 million'. The difference between the two estimates can be explained by the London insurance companies' determination to take note of bleach and printing works.[20] In 1834 capital invested in the finishing trades was equal to half that in spinning and weaving (see Table IV), and though there is no direct relationship between capital invested and value of output, it is reasonable to recognise this as a further indication of the importance of bleaching, dyeing and printing. Until more is known about the finishing trades it is not possible to be too emphatic, but it seems that Deane and Cole's figures may underestimate the contribution of the industry to the gross national product. If £20m is a realistic estimate of the gross value of output in 1797, value added was £17m, and cotton was already contributing over 7 per cent of the national income.

The importance of the subject and the doubts about the validity of Deane and Cole's figures have induced other econometric historians to enter the field. C. K. Harley has recalculated the size of the various sectors of the British economy from 1700 to 1841 by working back from the occupational data of the 1841 census of population, the earliest to provide comprehensive information. His new indices imply that eighteenth-century industry was nearly twice as large as previous estimates indicated so that its subsequent transformation was less dramatic than the phase 'Industrial Revolution' or Rostow's concept of it would suggest [73: 267–89].

The literary evidence surveyed in the earlier part of this book could offer some support for this interpretation in so far as there is ample evidence of a strong domestic industry and vigorous growth of the proto-factory in the eighteenth century, while the early cotton mills were on a more modest scale than the first generation of economic historians surmised. N. F. R. Crafts, in a difficult book on *British Economic Growth during the Industrial Revolution* (Oxford, 1985) has taken up Harley's work and incorporated it with a range of other econometric work to offer another interpretation of the process of economic growth. He agrees with Harley that earlier estimates 'exaggerate growth' and that some of Deane and Cole's estimates are 'implausible', but believes that 'It is the experience of the revolutionised cotton industry that stands apart' [70: 30–3]. In other words, we are back to an interpretation of British economic growth that assigns a unique role to cotton, albeit within a more gradual overall growth of the economy.

However, before rushing to embrace the latest thesis on offer, we should pause once again to check the supporting material. At the outset of his book, Crafts recognises that estimates of economic growth prior to the mid nineteenth century can never be more than 'controlled conjectures' [70: 9], though this does not restrain him and other econometricians from reaching some very firm conclusions from them. This is not the place to embark on any systematic assessment of this research, but so far as the cotton industry is concerned, it is worth noticing that Crafts simply adopts Deane and Cole's estimates, despite the criticism made in the first edition of this book in 1972 and despite his own trenchant criticism of other haphazard calculations. If Harley's estimates are combined with a much more realistic view of the growth of cotton than that offered by Deane and Cole and by Crafts, we should presumably conclude identifying an industry whose contribution to the economy appeared quite outstanding, or at any rate more than that so far recognised by any of them.

Fortunately the literary evidence is less confusing and offers some undisputed evidence of the wide-ranging contribution of cotton to the growth of the British economy between 1770 and mid nineteenth century. Arkwright's techniques were not difficult to apply to worsted spinning, and worsted mills modelled on his cotton mills were soon being built in the hosiery districts of the Midlands and in parts of Lancashire, the West Riding and Scotland

[9: *25–7*; 32: *75–95*]. Cotton displaced some fabrics formerly made in worsted, but the overall effect was to stimulate it, particularly for new lines such as carpets.[21] In the linen industry, John Marshall of Leeds inaugurated the factory system by adopting Arkwright's techniques and factory organisation.[22] Wool was unsuitable for roller spinning, but easily succumbed to the mule.[23] The hosiery and lace industries were still organised under a species of the domestic system, but benefited from cheaper and finer yarns. When the power loom won acceptance in cotton, it was soon being modified for wool, worsted, linen and silk yarns. If the cotton industry did not lead the national economy, it certainly led the British and (until the early 1830s) the European and American textile industry in its technology, in the development of the factory system, and in standardised production for the popular market.

It is also possible to demonstrate some direct connections between the cotton industry and the birth of new activities in other sectors of the economy. The first multi-storey cotton mills built in the 1790s introduced the idea of iron-framed buildings, a technical innovation with far-reaching consequences for architecture and the building industry. Early in the next decade these mills were among the first public buildings to be lit by gas, and the excitement with which contemporaries gazed at the illuminated mills guaranteed the spread of the technique [14: *Ch. 8*]. The early factory colonies introduced new standards of working-class housing which were widely copied in the surrounding areas and helped to effect a general improvement of housing standards in the Midlands and North of England.[24] The pioneers of factory production, Arkwright, Strutt, Peel and others, had to build most of their own plant, and in so doing established the practice of using specialised machinery for mass production of components such as spindles, rollers, gear wheels and bolts [43: *39*]. The idea of *standardised* production of cotton machinery was introduced in the 1830s by Richard Roberts, the Manchester inventor of the automatic mule, and was quickly carried over into other branches of engineering, such as the building of railway locomotives [12: *478*]. The earliest railway line built for regular passenger and goods services linked Liverpool and Manchester, and the first major phase of railway construction in the 1840s Lancashire investors contributed most of the capital.[25] Many of the ironfounding, engineering and chemical firms in Lancashire, the Glasgow region, the West Riding and the Vale of Trent (Nottingham region) owed their birth or growth to the enormous stimulus given to the regional economies during Rostow's 'take-off' period [12: Ch. 13; 26: 147–53]. These connections between cotton and other developments in the economy are clearly very important, but their development took place after the 'take-off' period, and they are not the same as the direct multiplier effect involved in the argument of Deane and Cole. However, they could reasonably be included in Rostow's definition of the 'forward effects' of the growth of the leading sector, a dimension that is practically impossible to measure.

The controversy that followed the publication of the Rostow thesis focused particular attention on the period between 1780 and 1880. One of the merits of Deane and Cole's work is that it identifies other periods of expansion, and draws attention to the 'peak period of growth' in cotton in the quarter-century after 1815, when raw cotton imports multiplied four and a half times. Data from Ellison, a well-informed nineteenth-century writer, have been reproduced by Deane and Cole to indicate that payments to labour (wages, salaries, etc.) took a falling percentage of the gross receipts of the cotton industry in the 1820s, 1830s and 1840s, and consequently they advance the suggestion that the spectacular growth of the quarter-century was financed by 'a marked increase in the share of profit in net output' [71: 189]. The point, if it can be substantiated, has important implications for the hotly debated issue of the standard of living, as well as for investment trends. However, business histories offer no support for this thesis. They show that Ashworth Brothers, M'Connel & Kennedy, and Kirkman Finlay, respectively leading cotton firms in Bolton, Manchester and Glasgow, were all experiencing falling profit margins in these decades. Lee concludes his study of M'Connel & Kennedy with the view that 'productivity did not increase quick enough in this period to offset the declining [raw] cotton/yarn price margin's effects' [39: 27–33; 46: 138–43]. Of course it might be argued that these three big firms were not representative of the whole industry. In the first half of the nineteenth century the average capacity of cotton mills increased thirteen times (see Table X) as the numerous small entrepreneurs struggled to assimilate the achievements of the pioneers of factory production, and it seems reasonable to suppose that rapid strides in efficiency were

Table X   Number and Average Size of Cotton Mills in Britain, 1797–1850

	No. of spinning factories	Approx. annual UK import of cotton (million lb)	Average annual input per factory (lb)
1797	c.900	30	33,000
1833–4	c.1,125	300	270,000
1850	1,407	600	430,000

Sources: Table III, and E. Baines, *History of the Cotton Manufacture* (1835) p. 394; B. R. Mitchell and P. Deane, *Abstract of British Historical Statistics* (1962) pp. 178–9.

accompanied by thin but improving profit margins. However, we must wait for some more business histories before this problem can be decided.

Turning from investment and production (the supply side) to domestic and overseas markets (the demand side), it is necessary first of all to emphasise that British superiority in quality production had secured a firm foothold in consumer tastes before the era of the great inventors. Until recently, the superiority of eighteenth-century French copperplate cotton prints was taken for granted, but the discovery of English pattern books with a wide variety of floral and pictorial designs of high quality has convinced art historians that London and Dublin, rather than Paris, perfected the techniques of designing, engraving and colouring of printed textiles in the third quarter of the eighteenth century. The history of the ceramic and fine metal industries in the English provinces is dominated by the names of Wedgwood and Boulton, entrepreneurs whose reputation and commercial success were based on the exploitation of a large variety of tastefully designed goods, and it is at least plausible that Lancashire's great achievement was based on comparable flair. However Lévy-Leboyer, a leading French economic historian, has won support for a theory suggesting that in the Industrial Revolution British cotton manufacturers concentrated on mass production, compelling the French producers to concentrate on quality [58: *175*]. Kusamitsu, a Japanese scholar, believes that the new type of British entrepreneur who rose to power in the period subverted the traditional craftsman-designer [61: *77–95*]. Most recently, the question has been taken up by British art historians who, concentrating on surviving fabrics rather than contentious literature of the period, have been impressed by the ingenuity of Lancashire textile printers and commended many of the designs which are far removed from the popular conception of Victorian drabness [59: 102–15; 60: 181–9]. Comparison of the careers of two leading Lancashire printers of the first half of the nineteenth century, James Thompson who concentrated on high-quality designed goods and John Brooks who produced large quantities of cheap imitations for the domestic and Indian markets, reveals the existence of high profits and catastrophic losses in both [58: 183–92]. Between them lay a whole range of printers specialising in particular markets, techniques or fashions, all more or less vulnerable to sudden shifts in demand from the fickleness of fashion or taste at home or abroad. In this period British textile producers were out to win the world market for both cheap mass-produced *and* quality fabrics, and to a remarkable degree they succeeded.

In practice the two aspects of consumer demand cannot be separated for, as the work on Wedgwood and Boulton illustrates, capturing the quality market is the key to large popular sales. A recent book on *The Birth of a Consumer Society* is a fresh reminder of the passion for novelty and buying that seized all classes in eighteenth-century England, and of the fluidity of a society in which constant changes in dress like all other material possessions, affected all ranks of society with remarkable speed.[26] Overseas trade was important to the modest industrial growth that was going on before the Industrial Revolution, but was not essential to the 'take-off' [51: 63]. The foundations of the success of cotton in the Industrial Revolution lay in a consumer society with seemingly unsatiable appetite for new fashion, and a corps of entrepreneurs with the ingenuity, versatility and resource to feed that demand and then to sustain the growth of the industry by increasing overseas sales, first in traditional markets and then in distant parts of the world.

References

1. M. T. Wild, 'The Saddleworth Parish Registers', *Textile History*, I (1969).

2. W. Radcliffe, *Origins of Power Loom Weaving* (Stockport, 1828), pp. 10, 65–6.

3. J. D. Chambers, *Nottinghamshire in the Eighteenth Century* (1932), Ch. 5.

4. W. H. Chaloner, *People and Industries* (1963), Ch. 1.

5. D. S. L. Cardwell, 'Power Technologies and the Advance of Science 1700–1825', *Technology and Culture*, VI (1965).

6. Calculations based on data in Notts CRO, Portland Mss DD4P 79/63, and Public Record Office (PRO) Chatham Mss 30/8/187.

7. Radcliffe, op. cit., p. 62.

8. James Montgomery, *Carding and Spinning Master's Assistant* (Glasgow, 1832), p. 170, and *A Practical Detail of the Cotton Manufacture in the USA . . . compared with that of Great Britain* (Glasgow, 1840) pp. 75–81; A. Ure, *The Cotton Manufacture of Great Britain* (1836), pp. 297–313.

9. E. Butterworth, *Historical Sketches of Oldham* (1856) pp. 140, 153, 183, shows that from 1821 to 1825 the number of cotton manufacturers rose from 60 to 139.

10. Notts CRO, DD4P 79/63.

11. PRO, B1/124, p. 21.

12. Abraham Rees, *Cyclopaedia*, article on 'Cotton' (*c.* 1808). S. D. Chapman, *The Devon Cloth Industry in the 18th C.* (Torquay, 1978), pp. xx–xxiii.

13. S. D. Chapman, *The Rise of Merchant Banking* (1984), Ch. 1.

14. C. Hulbert, *Memoirs of Seventy Years of an Eventful Life* (1852), p. 195.

15. A. Redford, *Labour Migration in England 1800–1850* (1926), Ch. 2.

16. Rees, *Cyclopaedia*, article on 'Cotton'.

17. S. Pollard, *The Genesis of Modern Management* (1965), Ch. 5.

18. S. D. Chapman, Introduction to G. J. French, *The Life and Times of Samuel Crompton* (1859; new edn, 1970), p. vi.

19. D. E. C. Eversley, 'The Home Market and Economic Growth in England, 1750–80', in E. L. Jones and G. E. Mingay (eds), *Land, Labour and Population in the Industrial Revolution* (1967).

20. PRO, Chatham Mss., 30/8/187.

21. Rees, *Cyclopaedia*, article on 'Worsted Manufacture' (*c.* 1818).

22. W. G. Rimmer, *Marshalls of Leeds, Flax Spinners* (1960).

23. D. T. Jenkins and K. G. Ponting, *The British Wool Textile Industry 1770–1914* (1982) pp. 110, 264–5.

24. S. D. Chapman, 'Workers' Housing in the Cotton Factory Colonies 1770–1850', *Textile History*, VII (1976).

25. S. Broadbridge, 'The Early Capital Market: the Lancashire and Yorkshire Railway', *Economic History Review*, VIII (1955–6).

26. N. McKendrick, J. Brewer and J. H. Plumb, *The Birth of a Consumer Society* (1982).

Select Bibliography

GENERAL WORKS

[1] E. Baines, *History of the Cotton Manufacture in Great Britain* (1835), 2nd edn (Cass, 1966). Now used only as a reference work, though quite readable.

[2] D. A. Farnie, *The English Cotton Industry and the World Market 1815–96* (Oxford, 1979). Concentrates on the structure of the industry and its world market; as the title implies, much of this book covers the period after the Industrial Revolution.

[3] M. Lévy-Leboyer, *Les Banques européenes et l'industrialisation internationale* (Paris, 1964). Includes valuable insights into British economic development, especially in textiles.

[4] G. Turnbull, *A History of the Calico Printing Industry in Great Britain* (Altrincham, 1951). Useful outline but parts of the book now superseded (see [43], [57]–[63]).

[5] A. P. Wadsworth and J. de L. Mann, *The Cotton Trade and Industrial Lancashire 1600–1780* (Manchester, 1931). Remains the standard work on the early period.

TECHNOLOGY

[6] C. Aspin, *James Hargreaves and the Spinning Jenny* (Helmshore, 1964). The best account of the inventor and his invention.

[7] H. Catling, *The Spinning Mule* (Newton Abbot, 1970). Historical perspective by a textile technologist; for an economist's view see [67].

[8] S. D. Chapman, 'The Cost of Power in the Industrial Revolution', *Midland History*, I (1970) 1–23. A study of Robinsons, the earliest firm to buy a steam engine for direct transmission to cotton-spinning machinery.

[9] S. D. Chapman 'The Arkwright Mills', *Industrial Archaeology Review*, VI (1981), 5–27. Describes the Arkwright prototype mill and revises the widely-quoted estimate of the number built by 1788 from 150 to over 200.

[10] H. J. Habakkuk, *American and British Technology in the Nineteenth Century. The Search for Labour-saving Inventions* (Cambridge, 1962). Classic study with valuable insights on the cotton industry.

[11] R. L. Hills, 'Hargreaves, Arkwright and Crompton. Why Three Inventors?' *Textile History*, X (1979), 114–26. Analyses the merits of the key inventions in layman's language.

[12] A. E. Musson and E. Robinson, *Science and Technology in the Industrial Revolution* (Manchester, 1969). Includes useful essays on the Lancashire chemical and engineering industries, showing how they grew out of the cotton industry.

[13] M. E. Rose, 'Samuel Crompton (1735–1827) Inventor of the Spinning Mule', *Transactions of the Lancashire and Cheshire Antiquarian Society*, LXXV (1965–6), 11–32. Brings G. J. French's biography, *Life and Times of Samuel Crompton* (1859), up to date.

[14] Jennifer Tann, *The Development of the Factory* (1970). Based on the valuable records of Boulton and Watt, the steam engine patentees who supplied many early cotton mills. Well illustrated.

[15] Jennifer Tann, 'Richard Arkwright and Technology', *History*, LVIII (1973) 29–44. Suggests that Arkwright's most original contribution was in production engineering, rather than spinning or mechanical power.

[16] G. N. Tunzelmann, *Steam Power and British Industrialisation to 1860* (Oxford, 1978). An econometric analysis of the adoption of steam power showing why water power was more widely favoured until so late as the 1840s.

CAPITAL

[17] M. Blaug, 'The Productivity of Capital in the Lancashire Cotton Industry during the Nineteenth Century', *Economic History Review*, 2nd ser., XIII (1961), 358–81. Assembles and analyses contemporary estimates for the period 1833 to 1886.

[18] S. D. Chapman, 'Fixed Capital Formation in the British Cotton Industry 1770–1815', *Economic History Review*, 2nd ser., XXIII (1970), 235–66. Synthesises new estimates of capital formation from fire insurance registers, explaining why fixed capital needs were lower than had been supposed.

An extended version of this essay, taking the analysis down to 1835, is in J. P. P. Higgins and S. Pollard (eds), *Aspects of Capital Investment in Great Britain 1750–1850* (1971), pp. 51–107.

[19] S. D. Chapman, 'Financial Restraints on the Growth of Firms in the Cotton Industry, 1790–1850', *Economic History Review*, XXXII (1979), 50–69. Argues that the numerous small firms and high mortality of firms typical of Lancashire cotton were consequence of long-term shortages of working capital.

[20] V. A. C. Gattrell, 'Labour, Power and the Size of Firms in Lancashire Cotton in the Second Quarter of the Nineteenth Century', *Economic History Review*, XXX (1977), 95–125. Assembles data to show the 'small to middling' size of most firms in Lancashire cotton at the period and considers some explanations.

[21] F. Stuart Jones, 'The Financial Needs of the Cotton Industry during the Industrial Revolution: A Survey of Recent Research', *Textile History*, XVI (1985), 45–68. A helpful guide to and summary of the debate.

[22] F. Stuart Jones, 'The Cotton Industry and Joint-Stock Banking in Manchester', *Business History*, XX (1978), 165–85. Chronicles the formation of Manchester banks.

[23] M. B. Rose, 'The Role of the Family in Providing Capital and Managerial Talent in Samuel Greg and Co 1784–1840', *Business History*, XIX (1977). A useful case-study illustrating some familiar features of the cotton industry at the period. See also [45].

[24] S. Shapiro, *Capital and the Cotton Industry* (Cornell, New York, 1967). Written before scholarly debate on the subject took off, this book is now mainly interesting for case-studies.

THE STRUCTURE OF THE INDUSTRY

(A) Interpretations

[25] S. D. Chapman, 'The Textile Factory before Arkwright: A Typology of Factory Development', *Business History Review*, XLVIII (1974), 451–78. Distinguishes the workshop, factory, and proto-factory, and compares their various fixed costs in the eighteenth century.

[26] S. D. Chapman, *The Early Factory Masters* (Newton Abbot, 1967). An analysis of the origins of enterprise and problems faced by cotton mill owners in the midland counties in the eighteenth century.

[27] J. H. Clapham, 'Some Factory Statistics of 1815–16', *Economic Journal*, XXV (1915), 475–9. Useful reference article.

[28] F. Crouzet, *The First Industrialists. The Problem of Origins* (Cambridge, 1985). The best contribution to the self-help debate; digests numerous studies of the cotton industry to demonstrate upward social mobility.

[29] G. W. Daniels, 'Samuel Crompton's Census of the Cotton Industry in 1811', *Economic History*, II (1930–3), 107–110. Useful reference article.

[30] K. Honeyman, *Origins of Enterprise, Business Leadership in the Industrial Revolution* (Manchester, 1982). Examines the origins of Arkwright-type mill owners and Bolton and Oldham mule spinners.

[31] A. Howe, *The Cotton Masters 1830–1860* (Oxford, 1984). The main focus of this work is political, but the first two chapters provide a valuable reconstruction of the second-generation 'millocracy'.

[32] D. T. Jenkins, 'The Cotton Industry in Yorkshire, 1789–1900', *Textile History*, X (1979), 75–95. Surveys a neglected area of the cotton industry.

[33] R. Lloyd-Jones and A. A. Le Roux, 'The Size of Firms in the Cotton Industry 1815–41', *Economic History Review*, XXXIII (1980), 72–82. Draws on Manchester rate books to emphasise the importance of middle- rather than small-sized firms; see also [19] and [20] for the debate on the size of firms.

[34] R. Lloyd-Jones and A. A. Le Roux, 'Marshall and the Birth and Death of Firms: the Growth and Size Distribution of Firms in the Early 19th Century Cotton Industry', *Business History* XXIV (1982), 140–55. Rejects Marshall's 'trees in the forest' concept of industrial growth as a model for understanding the early cotton industry.

[35] R. Lloyd-Jones and M. J. Lewis, 'The Economic Structure of "Cottonopolis" in 1815', *Textile History*, XVII (1986), 71–89. Examines Manchester warehouses in 1815 to make comparison with the scale of investment in mills.

[36] H. B. Rodgers, 'The Lancashire Cotton Industry in 1840',

Transactions of the Institute of British Geographers, XXVIII (1960), 135–53. Concentrates on the spatial distribution of the industry, complementing [37] and [38].

[37] A. J. Taylor, 'Concentration and Specialisation in the Lancashire Cotton Industry, 1825–50', *Economic History Review*, 2nd ser., I (1948–9), 114–22. Should be read in conjunction with [36] and [38].

[38] K. L. Wallwork, 'The Calico Printing Industry of Lancastria in the 1840s', *Transactions of the Institute of British Geographers*, XLV (1968), 143–56. Complements H. B. Rodger's analysis of the distribution of the cotton industry, focusing on the most important of the finishing branches.

(B) Case-studies of firms

[39] R. Boyson, *The Ashworth Cotton Enterprise* (Oxford, 1970). A valuable study of one of the best known second-generation firms.

[40] John Butt (ed.), *Robert Owen, Prince of Cotton Spinners* (Newton Abbot, 1971). A collection of essays on Owen and his famous community at New Lanark.

[41] W. H. Chaloner, 'Robert Owen, Peter Drinkwater and the Early Factory System in Manchester 1788–1800', *Bulletin of the John Rylands Library*, XXXVII (1954), 78–102. Provides the Manchester context of R. Owen, *Life of Robert Owen* (1854).

[42] S. D. Chapman, 'James Longsdon (1745–1821), Farmer and Fustian Manufacturer: the Small Firm in the Early English Cotton Industry', *Textile History*, I (1970), 265–92. Examines the problems of a typical small first-generation enterprise.

[43] S. D. Chapman and S. Chassagne, *European Textile Printers in the Eighteenth Century: A Study of Peel and Oberkampf* (1981). A comparative study of the most successful first-generation British and French factory owners in this branch of the cotton industry.

[44] R. S. Fitton and A. P. Wadsworth, *The Strutts and the Arkwrights* (Manchester, 1958). An outstanding business history, but now in need of some updating with more recent research.

[45] Mary B. Rose, *The Gregs of Quarry Bank Mill. The Rise and Decline of a Family Firm 1750–1914* (Cambridge, 1986). The

only history of a cotton dynasty, a nice introduction to the famous National Trust cotton mill village near Manchester.

[46] C. H. Lee, *A Cotton Enterprise 1795–1840: A History of M'Connel and Kennedy, Fine Cotton Spinners* (Manchester, 1972). Examines the valuable records of this important Manchester firm of mule spinners.

[47] Robert Owen, *Life of Robert Owen* (1857). The most illuminating autobiography covering the early years of the factory system in Lancashire and Scotland, but see also [40; 41].

[48] G. Unwin *et al.*, *Samuel Oldknow and the Arkwrights* (Manchester, 1924). A pioneer business history that is still important.

MARKETING

(A) Supply of cotton and selling organisation

[49] S. D. Chapman, 'The Foundations of the English Rothschilds: N. M. Rothschild as a Textile Merchant 1799–1811', *Textile History*, VIII (1977), 99–115. Case-study of Anglo-Continental trade.

[50] S. D. Chapman, 'The International Houses: the Continental Contribution to British Commerce 1800–1860', *Journal of European Economic History*, VI (1977), 5–48. Explains how and why textiles were marketed in Europe by firms of Continental origin.

[51] Ralph Davis, *The Industrial Revolution and British Overseas Trade* (Leicester, 1979). Recalculation of the volumes and values of British imports and exports in the period; indispensable.

[52] M. M. Edwards, *The Growth of the British Cotton Trade 1780–1815* (Manchester, 1969). Closely examines the commercial development of the industry during its most rapid period of growth.

[53] F. E. Hyde, B. B. Parkinson and S. Mariner, 'The Cotton Broker and the Rise of the Liverpool Cotton Market', *Economic History Review*, VIII (1955–6), 75–83. Revision of an early classic, T. Ellison's *Cotton Trade of Great Britain* (1886).

[54] J. R. Killick, 'Bolton, Ogden and Co: A Case Study in Anglo-American Trade 1790–1850', *Business History Review*, XLVIII (1974), 501–19. An American firm exporting cotton to Europe.

[55] A. Slaven, 'A Glasgow Firm in the Indian Market: John Lean and Sons, Muslin Weavers', *Business History Review*, XLIII (1969), 496–522. Informative case-study of the problems of supplying Britain's principal export market last century.

[56] D. M. Williams, 'Liverpool Merchants and the Cotton Trade 1820–1850' in J. R. Harris (ed.), *Liverpool and Merseyside* (1969), pp. 182–211. Measures the structure of the Liverpool mercantile community in its heyday.

(B) Consumerism and fashion

[57] Aileen Ribeiro, *Dress in Eighteenth Century Europe 1715–89* (1985). The best-informed of a range of costume histories.

[58] S. D. Chapman, 'Quality versus Quantity in the Industrial Revolution: the Case of Textile Printing', *Northern History*, XXI (1985), 175–92. Argues that the French by no means dominated the production of 'up-market' cotton prints [cf. 3: 60].

[59] H. Clark, 'The Design and Designing of Lancashire Printed Calicoes during the first half of the 19th Century', *Textile History*, XV (1984), 101–18. A fashion historian's view.

[60] D. Greysmith, 'Patterns, Piracy and Protection in the Textile Printing Industry', *Textile History*, XIV (1983), 163–94. The role of fashion design and plagiarism in cotton printing.

[61] T. Kusamitsu, 'British Industrialisation and Design before the Great Exhibition', *Textile History*, XII (1981), 77–95. Argues for deterioration in standards of British design in calico printing and other industries as a consequence of the factory system; for another view see [58] and [63].

[62] B.Lemire, 'Developing Consumerism and the Readymade Clothing Trade in Britain 1750–1800', *Textile History*, XV (1984), 21–44. Considers various factors in the demand side of the growth of the cotton industry.

[63] F. M. Montgomery, *Printed Textiles: English and American Cottons and Linens 1700–1850* (1970). An attractive survey of the early history of calico printing by an art historian.

LABOUR AND INDUSTRIAL RELATIONS

[64] M. H. Mackenzie, 'Calver Mill and its Owners', *Derbyshire Archaeological Journal*, LXXXIII (1963) 24–34. Arkwright-type factory colony with London connections.

[65] D. Bythell, *The Handloom Weaver* (Cambridge, 1969). Should
      be read in conjunction with E. P. Thompson, *The Making of the
      English Working Class* (1963), as explained in Section 5 of the
      text.

[66] Frances Collier, *The Family Economy of the Working Classes in the
      Cotton Industry* (Manchester, 1965). Analyses family income
      of employees in some early cotton mills.

[67] M. Cruickshank, *Children and Industry: Child Health and
      Welfare in North-West Textile Towns during the Nineteenth
      Century* (Manchester, 1981). Useful study of a large litera-
      ture.

[68] William Lazonick, 'Industrial Relations and Technical
      Change: The Case of the Self-Acting Mule', *Cambridge
      Journal of Economics*, III (1979) 231–62. Shows that mule
      spinners were an elite of skilled workmen, rather than an
      exploited proletariat; see also [7].

[69] Jean Lindsay, 'An Early Industrial Community. The Evans'
      Cotton Mill at Darley Abbey, Derbyshire 1783–1810',
      Business History Review, XXXIV (1960), 277–301. Useful case-
      study.

COTTON IN THE ECONOMY

[70] N. F. R. Crafts, *British Economic Growth during the Industrial
      Revolution* (Oxford, 1985). Contains a synthesis of recent
      econometric work on the industrial revolution, including
      [71] and [73], as well as the author's own research.

[71] P. Deane and W. A. Cole, *British Economic Growth 1688–1959*
      (Cambridge, 1967). Pioneer econometric work containing
      influential interpretations of the role of cotton at variance
      with those of Rostow [74].

[72] H. J. Habakkuk and P. Deane, 'The Take-off in Britain' in
      W. W. Rostow (ed.), *The Economics of Take-off into Sustained
      Growth* (1965). Criticises Rostow's assessment of the funda-
      mental role of cotton in the industrial revolution [see 74].

[73] C. K. Harley, 'British Industrialisation before 1841: evidence
      of slower growth during the Industrial Revolution', *Journal
      of Economic History*, XLII (1982) 267–89. Econometric analysis
      suggesting that the transformation of the industrial sector in
      eighteenth-century Britain was less dramatic than Rostow
      supposed [see 74].

[74] W. W. Rostow, *The Stages of Economic Growth* (Cambridge, 1960). An economist's concept of the process of industrialisation which assigns a central role to cotton in the case of Britain.

Index

Africa, 15, 41
Apprenticeship, 47
Aristocracy, 33
Arkwright (Sir) Richard, 15, 17–
19, 20–2, 31, 45, 47–8, 57–8,
65, 68
Arkwright-type mills, 27, 47, 58,
64
Ashworth Bros, 48, 59, 68

Banks, 34, 66
Blackwell Hall, 11–12
Bleaching, 23, 56

Calico printing, 12, 17, 28, 34,
56, 60–1, 64, 68
Capital, 12, 26–34, 65–6
Cartwright, Major John, 19, 24
Chemical Industry, 23, 58
Chintz, 15
Costs, of cotton yarns, 37, 53; of
power, 25
Cotton mills: building of, 58, 65;
cost of, 27; number of, 27–9,
60, 64–5; organisation of, 17,
20, 22, 47–9; size of, 24–5,
27, 60, 65
Credit, 12, 28, 32–4
Crises, commercial, 34, 42
Crompton, Samuel, 17, 20–1,
65, 67

Dale, David (& Co.), 28, 30, 47
Demand, see Exports, Home
Market
Discipline in factories, 14, 47–8
Domestic system, 13, 18, 50–2,
57–8

Douglas, William (& Co.), 21, 28,
30
Dutch engine loom, 12, 53

East India Co., 12, 15, 36
European Market, 41
Exports, 42–4, 60–1, 69–70

Factory colonies, 47–9, 58, 68–9
Factory system, 17, 20–1, 24–5,
58
Fairbairn, William, 24–5
Fashion, 16, 40, 60–1, 70
Framework knitting, 13–14, 23–
4, 51, 58
Fustian, 11–13

Gardom, Pares & Co., 33
Glasgow, 21, 23, 39, 45, 51
Greg, Samuel (& Co.), 45–7, 68

Handloom weavers, 13, 22–4,
50–2, 56, 71
Hargreaves, James, 17, 22, 27,
64
Home market, 15–16, 53, 60–1
Hosiery industry, see Framework
knitting
Housing, 58

Imports, of raw cotton, 38–9
Indian textile industry, 12, 15,
20
Iron industry, 54, 58–9

Jenny spinning, 17, 21, 27, 64

Kay, John, 53

Labour supply for mills, 45–8
Linen industry, 45, 58
Liverpool, 38–9
Livesey, Hargreaves & Co., 23, 34
Lombe, Thomas and John, 14
London, 11–12, 14, 16, 38–41, 47

Machine builders, 46
Manchester, 12, 23, 38–41, 45, 67
McConnel & Kennedy, 21, 30, 32, 39, 59, 69
Markets, for British cottons, 15–16, 41–4, 53, 60–1
Merchants, 14, 33–4, 38–42, 69–70
Millwrights, 46
Morley, I & R., 40
Mule Spinning, 21–1, 24–5, 49–50, 64, 71
Muslins, 21

New draperies, 11
Nottingham, 23, 39–40, 45

Oldknow, Samuel, 21, 31–2, 34, 40, 69
Owen, Robert, 30, 68–9

Peel, Robert (& Co.), 19, 21–2, 28, 31–2, 40, 48, 50, 58
Plantations, 15, 36
Power looms, 21, 24, 58
Prices, 25, 36–7, 39, 45
Productivity, 20, 59, 65
Profits, 31–2, 59–61
Proto-factory, 17, 57

Radcliffe, William, 13, 22, 24, 50
Railways, 58
Recruitment of labour, 45–7
Riots, 22
Roberts, Richard, 24–5, 58
Robinson & Co., 28, 31–2
Roebuck, Dr John, 23
Rostow, W. W., 54, 59, 72

Silk industry, 12, 14–15, 28, 58
Smiles, Samuel, 26
Social mobility, 26, 67
Steam power, 18–19, 24–5, 65
Stocking frame, 13–14, 53
Stockport, 15, 24, 45
Strutt, Jedediah (& Co.), 15, 21, 39, 47, 58, 68
Swiss industry, 21

Tennant, Charles, 23

United States, as a supplier of cotton, 36–9, 53; as a market, 41

Wages, 24, 45–9, 59
Wars, French, 28, 32, 34, 37–8, 41–2
Water power, 18–19, 24, 27, 45–7
Weaving, *see* Handloom weavers, Power looms
West Indies, 15, 36
Whitney's gin, 36
Woollen industry, 12, 28, 37–8, 58
Worsted spinning, 57–8